THE EYES
OF THE SHIP

Navigating the
Waters of Fatherhood

I trust this book will be a blessing to you!

JMoore
2/22/05

JIM MOORE

insight
PUBLISHING GROUP
Tulsa, Oklahoma

THE EYES OF THE SHIP

The Eyes of the Ship by Jim Moore
Published by Insight Publishing Group
8801 S. Yale, Suite 410
Tulsa, OK 74137
918-493-1718

All Scripture references are taken from the *Holy Bible: New International Version* (International Bible Society, East Brunswick, N.J.) 1984.

All of the information and research in this book pertaining to the Titanic, its passengers and crew, other ships and their passengers and crew, and anything pertaining to its history has been used from sources that are assumed to be truthful and accurate and has been used for example uses only, not factual content. The author and Mark IV, Inc. make no guarantees to the accuracies of it.

ISBN 1-932503-17-X
Library of Congress catalog card number: 2004101277

Printed in the United States of America

DEDICATION

Every man is created with two distinct needs: the need of a loving family and the need for a dedicated father. I have been blessed beyond measure to possess both.

This book is dedicated to my wife Liz—whose mission in life is to be the wife and mother she was created to be—and to our children, Ryan, Lauren, and Madison, who make the joy of fathering come easily every day.

This book is also dedicated to my father Louie Moore, who shows his family what a father should be every day.

TABLE OF CONTENTS

Dedication
Foreword
Preface
Introduction

Chapter One
The Collision in the Dark
19

Chapter Two
Unheeded Warnings That Led to Disaster
23

Chapter Three
The Curse
31

Chapter Four
Lessons Learned from the Titanic
41

Chapter Five
They Paid Little Attention to the Warning Signs
51

Chapter Six
*How You Drive the Ship Determines
How You Will Finish the Journey!*
61

Chapter Seven
Wrong Priorities Will Lead to a Shipwreck
69

Chapter Eight
*Sticks and Stones Can Break My Bones
But Words—They're a Real Killer*
79

Chapter Nine
What Was Supposed to Save It Actually Sank It
87

Chapter Ten
Turn Back Before the Screams Die Out
99

Chapter Eleven
When Dad's Not There
109

Chapter Twelve
Two Dads—Two Destinies
119

Chapter Thirteen
Lifesaving Lessons
129

FOREWORD

Jim Moore's book, *The Eyes of the Ship*, is inspirational! Building off one of the worst tragedies of the twentieth century he challenges us to realign our priorities as dads or our children will suffer. Moore's strong commitment to strengthening our schools is well respected. His pioneering work through an organization he founded named *Watch D.O.G.S.* fulfills the premise of his book, by engaging in responsible action. As a fellow father, you'll find his writing style will motivate you to excellence. I heartily recommend his book.

Ken R. Canfield, Ph.D.
President
National Center for Fathering

PREFACE

See if you've ever heard of this story: it's the account of a luxurious cruise ship around the turn of the twentieth century that struck an iceberg on its starboard side and sank, taking with it some of the world's most elite to their deaths. It was a ship that was designed to be unsinkable. It was a ship that was the most luxurious of its time, and no one thought a tragedy such as that could have ever happened to it.

We all know the name of it, don't we? Sure we do. It's the story of *Titanic*, right? Wrong! This story is actually describing a ship called the *Titan*. It was a fictional story written by a man named Morgan Robertson, and believe it or not, he wrote it in 1898—fourteen years before *Titanic* set sail on its maiden voyage.

It's uncanny and to some maybe a little eerie how the story of the *Titan* and the *Titanic* parallel each other so closely. Not only by their names but in just about every other way you can imagine. They were approximately the same size. They both had the capacity to carry about the same number of passengers and about the same number of lifeboats—the latter number proving woefully inadequate to both. Both ships were capable of about the same top speed. Both were equipped with the same number of propellers and almost the same number of bulkheads. Both had the same glamorous start and the same tragic finish. People thought them to be unsinkable, yet both sunk. They even sank in the same month!

In short, these ships were almost identical. The main difference was that one came from a man's imagination while the other was a real tragedy played out in front of the eyes of the whole world. It's enough to make you wonder how this kind of thing could happen—was the author of the book writing prophetically, or was it just a bizarre coincidence?

Whether prophetic or coincidental, Robertson's story of the *Titan* bears remarkable resemblance to the real-life story of the *Titanic's* tragedy fourteen years later. No one can argue with the reality of this strange similarity, and this leads me to the truth and the reason for this book.

Around 400 B.C., a man named Malachi prophesied that unless fathers turn their hearts back to their children and children back to their fathers, the land would come under a curse. Notice he named the fathers first and the responsibility fell squarely on the shoulders of us as dads. It is our obligation dads to pursue a relationship with our children, regardless of their age or ours, so they in turn would desire a relationship with us that is greater than any we could ever imagine!

Tragically, it's not happening today. All you have to do is to take a bird's-eye view of this world and the state of the modern-day family and you'll quickly get your answers. Kids today are caught up and trapped in deadly vices more than ever. Study after study shows that when a father isn't connected and committed to his children, they are more prone to violence, drugs, gang activity, poor grades, sexual promiscuity, depression, poverty, and countless other problems.

And these aren't skewed studies by groups with political agendas. Many kids without a committed father in their corner are struggling, and it's going to take an active reversal in the trend of uninvolved fathers to change the situation. Dads and positive male role models need to rise up and assume their God-given responsibilities for our children's future!

This call for fathers to return to their children is the reason for this book. Whether we like the idea or not, we men had better get back to the basics of life with our family. That means that we need to take our role as dads very seriously, or our kids, our culture, and ultimately our country will continue its rapid pace of neglect and ultimate destruction.

Jim Moore
2004

INTRODUCTION

I had just finished speaking to a group of educators about the content of this book, and I was preparing to leave the building and head back to my family when a woman in tears approached me.

She began to share that she had been crying throughout much of my entire speech. She began to tell me about her life and said that she believed everything I had said. This young woman told me the life of her daughter had painfully flashed before her eyes during my speech. She shared something that really gripped my heart—that her husband had left her and their daughter years ago and that the girl, now seventeen, was about to give birth to a baby. As this broken young woman told me this last part, she began to cry even harder.

Her comments and her pain caught me off guard and moved me so much that I really didn't know what to say to her then. But now I do. I want to tell her how thankful I am that she confided in me about her hurts and for being so brave and raising her daughter alone. I'd tell her—and anyone else in her situation—that though her task is formidable, it's not impossible. And it had to be done, with or without the girl's father, but it is my desire that this book can in some small way help her and other people in similar situations.

Though I hope this book will help the entire family, the crux of this book is to men. My hope is that it might help prevent these and other heartbreaking testimonies. This book is in no way against single mothers or demeaning women's role in any way, shape, or form, and nothing in this book is designed to portray mothers as weak or desperate. However, I will

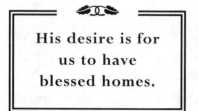

His desire is for us to have blessed homes.

unapologetically say that God's perfect plan for the family is for both mom and dad to raise children and build the family together. His desire is for us to have blessed homes, and I believe active fathers are vital to this process. Yet all too often, dads find themselves disconnected and disengaged, and that's the focus of this book.

On another occasion, I was speaking at a conference in a breakout session. Before my presentation, I decided to drop in and listen to the morning's keynote speaker. In the world's eyes this person speaking would be considered someone of prominence. The novelty of seeing and hearing her speak intrigued me, so I thought I would pop in for her speech. I believe the topic had something to do with parental involvement in the lives of children—specifically from an educator's point of view.

At least I thought that's what I would hear. What I actually witnessed was venom with an agenda. She began to attack fathers and their roles in the family, and she did it so much that my emotions went from simmering to boiling in a very short time. It got so bad that her speech literally turned vulgar, and it was at that time I made my exit to the door.

I thought of the words of the great philosopher Popeye the Sailor: "I had all I can stands, I can't stands no more!" I couldn't take any more of her attack against fathers! So I left, utterly disgusted at what I had seen and heard.

Do you realize, men, that there are factions that are small but loud and would silence fathers as a voice in society forever! I hope you realize this *really* is the case. Yet the world is looking for and has long been waiting for men to rise up and be what God created us to be.

My passion is that this book goes out as a challenge to men and inspires and encourages us to stand up. Perhaps now more than ever before, fathers need to rise up and positively influence our culture. We've got to step up to the responsibility to lead,

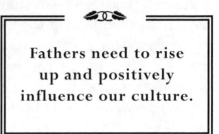

Fathers need to rise up and positively influence our culture.

equip, and inspire our families, as we are called to do, and we've got to stop listening once and for all to all the naysayers who falsely prophesy that men reclaiming our rightful place can't or shouldn't be done.

Our nation and the world are desperately looking for leaders for the home, and they will go to great lengths to find and follow those who can get the job done. Just as we as humans will invariably follow smoke to see what's burning or follow a spotlight in the sky to see where it's coming from, so people will travel great lengths and overcome huge obstacles to find the source of energy and light.

Dads, that's us! We really can be that light but we have to ask ourselves if we're willing to pay the price of selflessness and servanthood that will enable us to shine and make our families proud to call us "dad."

I'm really tired of seeing fathers and their children rapidly grow apart. I'm tired of seeing dads sheepishly relinquishing their responsibilities to someone or something else without ever taking a stand for their relationship with their children. I'm tired of a dark world with all of its cultural vices daily ensnaring families to the point that broken families are more common than whole ones. And I'm tired of seeing all these men—including myself—whose hearts have not taken hold of their destiny.

Something has to change, and I want it to start now, in me. And as you read this, hopefully it will begin in you as well.

I've written this book in the hopes that it will help all of us and our families. The time is short, and I'm also tired of wasting it so I'm on a journey to possess what is mine, and I'm going to try to take as many men with me as will go. Some may come quietly, and some might come kicking and screaming; it makes no difference to me, as long as we get there as quickly as possible.

So let's get going; the clock is ticking, and I promise you that the enemies of the family and strong fathers haven't been wasting time, so we shouldn't either! Let's get going before it's too late.

*What is it that makes mankind
get in a hurry when it's too late
to try to hold onto things that they
hope will help them float, when they
had plenty of time to stand on things
that would have let them live?*

CHAPTER ONE

THE COLLISION IN THE DARK

It was a Sunday night. Not just any Sunday night either. No sir, this one was going down in history as one for the ages. It was April 14, 1912, around 10:00 P.M. in the North Atlantic. The sky absolutely sparkled that evening. It was cloudless but without moonlight, yet well illumined by the stars.

There were over 2200 people on a journey together. Some were strolling around looking at the clear sky, all having their own conversations about various things. Some probably talked about the excitement of seeing their family and friends within a few days, while others likely discussed the thrill of a fresh start, a new life in a different country. No doubt most were in awe to be aboard such an incredible vessel, and although conversations and people were all different, they all had one common thread: they were about to become a part of history.

They were the first to embark on the maiden voyage on the ship of the ages, the RMS *Titanic*. The descriptive words about this ocean liner were just about as numerous as the people on board. It was tagged a dream-ship, unsinkable, one of a kind, a masterpiece. From the richest of the rich to those who spent most of what they possessed to just get on board, the passengers were experiencing something very special. Yet before the sun came up the next morning, every single life on board would be changed forever.

Titanic's arrival at New York was to be the most grandiose entrance to a ship's port of all time, but its destiny was cut short because of misfortune and carelessness.

The same can be said about the modern-day family. Many people have high expectations about creating a great home, yet somehow we fathers have become distracted and have lost our edge. Many chose to focus on something else for a short time, and now their homes are taking on water; and they're looking for that lifeboat to rescue their family.

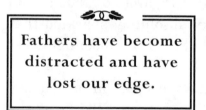

Fathers have become distracted and have lost our edge.

Something is missing, and many men sense it! Maybe this describes you, because you're no longer physically or emotionally connected to your spouse or your kids, and it seems as if your home can never get back to where it once was or where you so desperately want it to be. Or maybe you're on the opposite side of the coin. You're blessed and find yourself at what seems to be the pinnacle of a successful family, and you simply want to make sure you navigate and correctly avoid all the icebergs and pitfalls this world has to offer.

Most likely, you're somewhere in between. Whatever side of the pendulum you find yourself on, please don't let a tragedy become or even remain your story. Please don't let your and your family's future become destined to fail because of your inattention or neglect. Too much is at stake, dads, and it's going to take our whole hearts being turned toward what is right, and it's going to take us being determined to make the right choices, in order to survive all the icebergs that lie in wait for us and our home.

Remember, the iceberg the *Titanic* struck was just floating in the ocean. It had no compass or course. It was just there waiting to either be passed by or struck, and it was *the ship*, with all its talent and technologies, that failed. So it is with our families, dads. If we stay alert and on the right course, we can avoid the icebergs lying in wait for our families; and when we're successful, we never have to lower the lifeboats.

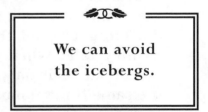

We can avoid the icebergs.

Men, let's not settle for failure! Let's settle for the destiny that can be ours. It might not always seem easy, but the safe arrival into our destined port will be worth it. So come on. Let's get started. Turn the page!

ACTION POINTS

1. Have you been careless with your family? If the answer is even close to "yes," then stop whatever you're doing right now and spend some constructive time with them—do whatever they're doing with them! And do it as soon as you're done with this chapter!

2. Do you feel as though you've lost the "edge" in your fathering skills? If so, begin changing that now. Ask your children how their day at school went before you do anything else after getting home from work today. Turn off the television and your phone, and just listen as they share with you all about their day. And don't forget to look them square in their eyes as they talk! When they're finished telling you about their day, ask them if you can do the same thing tomorrow—and then be sure and follow through with it!

3. Do you just sense that something is missing in your family? If this is true, then take the time to have a family meeting and air any conflicts that are going on—and do it before today ends. One word of warning: you might not like everything you hear, so make sure your heart is prepared to make some needed changes!

CHAPTER TWO

UNHEEDED WARNINGS
THAT LED TO DISASTER

Stop, close your eyes and listen. Can you hear it? Listen closely as the North Atlantic water breaks on both sides of the bow of the majestic cruiser. Listen as the band plays familiar tunes in the background. Husbands and wives talk about their thrilling journey while fathers and their children have probably said their goodnights to each other not knowing that for many it would be their last time to do so. The ship's crew is just getting settled in for what they hope is a peaceful and uneventful night's voyage.

It's 10:00 P.M., and *Titanic* is about 450 miles southeast of Newfoundland, but the people onboard aren't concerned about nautical miles, time, or directions. They are just excited to be a part of the greatest maiden voyage since Noah boarded his vessel thousands of years earlier.

The night is cold yet clear as two of the crewmen prepare to go to work. Their names are Reginald Lee and Frederick Fleet. Their job is to be the watchmen in a crow's nest on the ship. They are responsible for providing warning and protection for over 2200 people aboard the ship. Their duty is to report in a timely fashion anything that might bring harm to the vessel and its occupants. Their charge is to be the "eyes of the ship."

These two men climbed the pole to take their place in the crow's nest—and in history. But one thing they didn't take with them was a set of "glasses," which we now call binoculars. Apparently there were none to be found, though they had them at some point in the voyage. At some point this critical tool disappeared, and two generations of talk and second-guessing has mulled over why a ship of this prestige and magnitude would have been without such an important necessity. The largest, most luxurious ship in the world failed to offer the most basic, elementary form of security and safety for its passengers—a pair of binoculars.

There were no glasses for the lookouts. Think

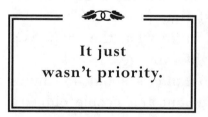

It just wasn't priority.

about this for a second. Can you imagine not having headlights for your car on a dark highway, not having a lighthouse beacon on a rocky shore, or not having a warning siren from an impending storm?

Well, like many others, this is my chance to express my opinion as to why it happened; and after reading many accounts of the fateful night, the conclusion I draw is simple. It was not intentional neglect or a shrouded coverup. There was no mysterious disappearance. You ready? Here's my take—*it just wasn't priority.* It failed to rank as significant. After all, wasn't this the same ship that some said was unsinkable? This was the same ship that some people said even God couldn't sink. What arrogance!

Something as simple as binoculars just wasn't that important. It was not a big deal. But as history proved, all of those foolish claims were flat-out wrong, and for want of something as simple as binoculars, the *Titanic's* voyage ended in tragedy.

There were many tragedies that came from the sinking of *Titanic.* Over fifteen hundred tragedies, actually, but possibly the greatest one of all was the fact that this disaster should have never happened!

Most people don't know that on that particular Sunday, the *Titanic* received no fewer than *six* messages from other ships warning the liner of potential danger and the need for caution.

They started coming around 9:00 that morning as the *Coronia* reported "growlers" and "fields of ice." Next came warnings from the *Noordam,* the *Baltic,* and the *Amerika.* Next came word from the *Californian* and finally the *Mesaba.*

Six warnings! Six times other ships took the time to notify this great vessel of the need for caution and for attention, but they simply went unheeded. Nothing major seemed to change. Not the course and certainly not the speed. Then at approximately 11:00 P.M., the *Californian* once again radioed the *Titanic,* attempting to tell them of their own position and predicament.

They transmitted, "Say, old man, we are stopped and surrounded by ice," to which the radio transmission reply from the *Titanic* came back, "Keep out! Shut up! I am busy, I am working Cape Race." Now stop for a moment and think about what they said.

Ship after ship did their nautical duty to warn this imperial vessel of the dangers that lay ahead in those precollision hours. But for some strange reason—most of which remain some two and a half miles under water to this day—*Titanic* continued on its deadly course into an ice field without even binoculars for safety.

Approximately forty minutes after the *Californian's* transmission, with the water temperature around thirty-one degrees, Frederick Fleet saw that the ship was headed for a dark mass. He immediately knew what it was, and you can bet he instantly knew what was about to happen. He picked up the phone, called down to the bridge, and uttered three infamous words that are etched forever in history books: "Iceberg right ahead!"

He received the response, "Thank you." They took evasive action, beginning a hard turn to port. But though the 882-foot-long vessel tried to turn away from disaster with all her might, she struck along an iceberg and opened a long gash in the hull.

About now you may be wondering, "Wait a minute! What in the world does this have to do with families—especially fathering—or reconnecting dads and their kids?"

It has everything to do with it, because this tragic story simply parallels what happens far too often in men's lives. Unprepared, rushed, and negligent attempts at fathering leave us with our families hanging in the balance.

I'm not trying to be judgmental or critical about the *Titanic's* decisions and therefore its disaster, and I only share this story because it brings to mind the disasters happening in so many families today. Dads are ignoring the warnings and not paying attention to the basics. Their inattention to the important things and their failure to clearly listen and make any and all necessary changes in their lives and ways can spell disaster for their families.

Our families—and therefore our culture—are suffering in a huge way because fathers have become scarce in this generation. I'm sure there's a lot of philosophies that attempt to curb the family deficits in our system and to reconnect dads and kids, but

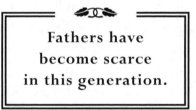

Fathers have become scarce in this generation.

many of them are reactionary. They often just seek to treat the pain without curing the cause, and many times by then, it's too late.

In today's real world, where kids are abandoned, neglected, hurt—or even worse— there are an awful lot of weak answers out there. They are proposed by those people whose agendas are not rooted in a solid foundation or grounded in sound wisdom and whose answers to the problems facing families comes up lacking when it comes to real solutions and to healing real hearts. When your family is on the line, the last thing you want to listen to (much less hook up with) is someone or something whose answers to your problems are anemic at best. You don't need their formula for success, which includes everything *except* helping us do the most important thing of all—looking into our inner selves and making whatever corrections in our own hearts and souls that are necessary before we can change our families. We need—no, we *must*—seriously seek out those who can truly provide the answers for which we're so desperately looking.

We fathers need to get ahead of the wave; we need to be preventative and proactive instead of reactionary, because we live in a world where families falling apart seems to be the norm and not the exception. If we've waited until we're in the middle of a field of icebergs at night, traveling at top speed, and we're not being an effective lookout for our family, we've waited too long. Many times families can't turn on a dime; it takes time.

It's time for us as fathers to wake up to the reality of fatherhood. It's time for men all over the world to live up to the incredible responsibility placed on us. It's time for the eyes of the ship to start functioning properly.

ACTION POINTS

1. Are you awake to the fact that YOU are the "eyes of the ship" in your home? You are! Right now, sit down and try to list three things in your family that you think your fatherly leadership could affect positively. Don't worry about how yet, just identify them. We'll get to "how" later.

2. Is there anything missing in your own heart that will cause your family to crash and sink? Right now, begin to do some serious self-examination. Begin by listing some items in your childhood that you don't want your children to have to experience.

3. Are you disregarding any warning signs that might be attempting to save you and your family? Take a moment to think of anything you have heard from teachers or your friends or others that could be warning signs for your children.

4. Is there a family that you know of that has or is breaking apart? Do you see any similarities between where they were when it began to break apart and where you are now? If so, then immediately begin to change the direction you and your family are headed, by getting focused on your home *now*. Begin by talking with your family. Express your concerns with them. You might be surprised that they possess some of the same concerns and may even have answers.

CHAPTER THREE

THE CURSE

If you ever choose to study about the causes of *Titanic's* tragic ending, chances are you'll come across some theories about why this incredible ship failed so miserably. Some are so far out in right field they are almost laughable. In one example I read, some people actually believed there was a mummy on board *Titanic* that carried with it some sort of curse! Creepy? No! Stupid? I think so!

But here's a curse that not only was prophesied some 2400 years ago, but one that has hit many families and homes with pinpoint accuracy. This curse really is looming in our world. At first, like many things it was subtle and quiet, but it has quickly raised its voice, and far too many homes have been wrecked by it. This affliction is rapidly spreading like wildfire throughout our culture at an alarming rate, and unless it is stopped it will continue to wipe out families by the millions.

It's the curse of inattention and abandonment. We have planted these destructive seeds in our children's lives for too long, and our nation and our world are reaping the harvest of fatherless families.

The only way we are going to be able to fix it is to attack it head-on and get to the core of the problem. We've got to defeat it, remove it, and then let the healing process begin in order to make the ultimate goal of "wholeness" become a reality in families.

Dad, whether you're a great father, a poor one, one who is there physically but not emotionally or one who isn't even around, your heart needs to turn back to your children! Wherever you are with your children, whatever stage you're both in, and however far you might have gone down the wrong path, turn around.

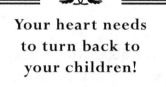

Your heart needs to turn back to your children!

There is a term that we are all too familiar with in our society. It's the expression "fatherless." It carries with it such a disturbing blemish, but I want to change the focus of that word for a very important reason. In some of my conversations and dialogue with Dr. Ken Canfield of The National Center for Fathering, he has stressed that the term "fatherless" is an unfair representation to most children's circumstances. No longer should we use the term "fatherless" but rather the expression we should be applying is the word "unfathered," and here's why.

The term "fatherless" denotes that maybe somewhere along the line the child might have been at fault or even played a part in determining their circumstances, when in reality many times it is the father's choice to abandon and to disregard the home that has placed the child in that condition. "Fatherless" might suggest it was the child's fault but being "unfathered" places the responsibility squarely on the shoulders of the one that in many cases made that choice—the father.

The Danger

This issue of abandonment and neglect is subtle, dangerous, and shrewd. Like a thief it can sneak up on people without them ever being aware of it. It's easy to start out on your journey with some of the greatest intentions in the world for your home only to look up one day and find that your ship is so far off course that it seems hopeless.

It's called drifting. The word itself has such a deceptive and insidious tone to it. Furthermore, it can happen to anyone and is already happening to far too many.

You've seen those dads; heaven knows, you might already be one. They're good guys, have great intentions, and are hard at work trying to make a good living for their families. And then one day, you look up and you're losing ground at such a rapid pace that it seems hopeless that you could ever recover from the "drift."

We'll talk later on how you can take some serious steps on reconnecting with your kids, but for now I want to focus on those just waking up to the drift, and especially to those who don't even realize what's happening.

What You Don't Know Will Hurt You—and Them

A prophet named Hosea once penned some of the wisest words ever written. He said that people are destroyed because of a "lack of knowledge." Did you catch that, dad? He didn't say it was a lack of money, a good job, or a lack of time or talent. It's a lack of knowledge!

Hosea's thought was that destruction, no matter how great or small, can always be traced to a lack of knowledge. He didn't say it's the lack of education, either, because you can definitely have the one without the other.

It's about being on the right or wrong path, and dads, let's face it, sometimes we are prone to drift off of the right path and onto the wrong one without ever knowing it, because many times we get so focused on our own agendas that we lose sight of the right priorities.

Now before you pass that thought off, consider this. Would you ever attempt to fly a plane without extensive training? Could you possibly teach a premed

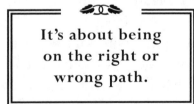

> It's about being on the right or wrong path.

class about kinesiology without formal preparation and a degree? Could you go to the local hardware store, buy a couple of hammers, a ton of nails, lumber, shingles, and build your dream house? Want to attempt an appendectomy without years of medical school, resident training, and special surgery training?

Then why do we think we can plant seeds of slothful fathering and never really know our kids and yet expect to harvest a normal, healthy, whole child? It starts with knowing truth, then it has to do with knowing your children (and them knowing you). And it's going to take us gaining the knowledge needed to accomplish the task.

In October 1999, The National Center for Fathering conducted a nationwide poll to determine how men across our nation were doing when it came to fathering. The issues they examined dealt with things such as the level of involvement in the child's learning. Questions ranged from, "How often do you take your child to school?" to issues such as, "How often do you attend parent/teacher conferences?" It was about simple stuff in which most fathers you would think should excel.

Questions were asked about a number of different situations, with the answers ranging from "every day," to "once or twice a week," to "once or twice a month," to "once every three months," to "never." Tragically, in nine out of thirteen questions asked, the response "never" was the most often given answer or a very close second. Take a look at it yourself.

1. How often (do you/does your child's father):*
- Every day
- Once or twice a week
- Once or twice a month
- Once every 3 months
- Never
- Don't know

1. Walk or take your child to school.
2. Visit your child's classroom.
3. Have lunch with your child at school.
4. Attend school meetings.
5. Attend class events.

6. Volunteer at your child's school.
7. Read to your child.
8. Help your child with homework.
9. Praise and reward your child for good schoolwork.
10. Help your child in extracurricular activities like music, sports, etc.
11. Meet with other dads for support.
12. Discuss your child's progress in school with your child's mother.
13. Communicate with your child's teacher.

2. How often (do you/does your child's father):*
- ■ Always
- ■ Sometimes
- ■ Never
- ■ Don't Know

1. Review and sign your child's report cards
2. Attend parent/teacher conferences
3. Attend school-based parents' organization meetings

3. Please answer "yes" or "no" to the following:*

1. Do you/does your child's father believe your child is getting a good education? ❑ Yes ❑ No
2. Are you/is your child's father confident that your child is safe at school? ❑ Yes ❑ No
3. Do you/does your child's father know the name of your child's physician? ❑ Yes ❑ No
4. Have you/has your child's father discussed school safety issues with your child? ❑ Yes ❑ No
5. Do you/does your child's father know the name of your child's teacher? ❑ Yes ❑ No

6. Have you/has your child's father helped your child complete a school project in the last six months?
❑ Yes   ❑ No

7. Do you/does your child's father know the name of the school counselor?   ❑ Yes   ❑ No

(*Fathers were asked the questions, "Do you..." Mothers were asked the questions, "Does your child's father...")

Take the test yourself. See just how well you do. I'll never forget the time I was sitting in a hotel room preparing to train men on fathering issues and decided that I had better see how well my score would stack up. Well, after taking the same test I would administer just a few hours later, I was somewhat embarrassed and taken aback. By the look of my own test score, it appeared that there were some questions for which I had obviously not studied.

Remember men, it's called the "drift." It's not called the "plunge," or the "rush," or the "haste." It's the drift. Webster's defines it as, "to vary or deviate from a set course or adjustment," or to "move along a line of least resistance," to "become carried along subject to no guidance or control." I believe the latter definition fits best because it speaks volumes of what happens most of the time. Seeds of abandonment and inattention, cultivated with no guidance or control, and you will harvest an "unfathered" child.

All across this nation and the world, men have fallen prey to this silent killer of relationships as day after day they are bombarded with cultural temptations to climb the corporate ladder or lay claim to trophy after trophy while their families wait for them to fulfill their God-given role. The rest of the family is left with the task of picking up the leftover crumbs dad scatters as he continues his breakneck pace to accomplish the illusive feat of becoming king of his mountain. Tragically, far too many times it takes some sort of shipwreck before dad wakes up to the fact that the greatest accomplishment he can achieve is to have a "whole" relationship with the ones closest to him.

In his book *The Name of the Game*, Steve Schall recounts the time he saw William Bennett on a late night talk show. William Bennett holds the distinguished credentials of having served as Drug Czar and Secretary of Education of the United States. As he was being introduced by the talk show host, Bennett said something amazing. I will paraphrase his comments. The talk show host said that he really didn't know how to introduce him since protocol dictated that he introduce him by his highest title he ever held, and since he had held two very distinguished titles, he was confused how to address him. Bennett answered by saying if he were going to address him by his highest honor or title, then he needed to just call him "dad."

Dads, we too need to wake up to the wonderful truth that the highest title our family can bestow upon us is still "dad."

So, how did you do on the test? You took it, didn't you? If you didn't, do not go one page further before you back up, answer the questions, and be totally honest with yourself. If you took it, what was the outcome? Does it look like you studied? Were you prepared, or were you like the multitudes that have just now realized that the clock is ticking and you only get one shot at today—that's all!

Now dads, we're at a crucial point here. It's at this point that some sort of early decision has to be made. Do you put down the book, go back to your regular way of being "dad" and hope that no shipwreck occurs; or do you need to ask yourself some serious and sometimes difficult questions such as, "What am I really doing?" or, "What's really important to me and my family, and what's really fluff?" And most of all, ask yourself, "What changes do I need to make to catch up for some lost time and to change the future for the best?"

You've probably heard that the definition of insanity is doing the same old thing over and over again and expecting different results. If you've been trying the same things repeatedly but you expect it to work, it just won't happen. Men, we are the prophets of our own lives, and our choices determine what type of dad we are and family we will have. So come on. Let's dig in and make sure there are no curses on this cruise.

ACTION POINTS

1. Make a list of people you know that you think might make good fathering mentors, and then think of something you might have in common with each of them that will help you connect to them and learn from them. Call and at least talk to one of them today!

2. Did you take the test, and if so did you pass it? If not, then use those questions as a study guide for what you should know about your family. Make a list of the top five you didn't know and focus on these, starting today!

3. Are there any activities that you've missed with your kids that you need to apologize for missing? If so, then make that call to your children now, regardless of their age!

CHAPTER FOUR

LESSONS LEARNED
FROM THE *TITANIC*

For the rest of our journey, I want to take a closer look at the largest peacetime nautical disaster and examine it. Let's see what really happened that fateful night as so many lost their families and their lives, and then let's check ourselves and our families out to determine how we stack up to see if there are any similarities between *Titanic's* last hours and our own home. Finally, we'll determine what actions we must take to try to keep our lives, families, and destinies from suffering some of the same pain and devastation that so many families have already experienced. And if by chance you're already in the water, clinging to anything that floats, my hope is that you will hear the heart of this book and diligently apply these truths in your life.

Dad, there are some incredible lessons we can learn from the time *Titanic* set out until it settled on the bottom of the ocean. Here's the first one:

Anything Man-Made is Sinkable

It was going to be a terrific Saturday. The Moore family, at that time just Liz and myself, were about to enjoy an incredible day of fun in the sun with a friend of mine from college, his wife, and their children. We were going to the lake for the first time out this particular summer on the Moore Family pontoon boat!

During my friend's college days in the late seventies, he was the starting center for our college basketball team. He stands 6'11" and his wife is close to 6' herself. I'm 6'2" and my wife is over 5'11" So our boat was filled with a bunch of tall people. We would have made a great coed volleyball team!

To say that we were excited was an understatement, because this was going to be an incredible time of food, fellowship, swimming, and lots of fun. We loaded their kids, the food, the chairs, the coolers, and just about everything else you can imagine in the front of the boat. Notice I said the *front* of the boat.

Now I'm a nautical amateur, and you can add to it that I'm also part of the male gender. You know the one I'm talking about—the kind that expects to find the boat in exactly the same condition that I left it in eight months earlier at the end of the last summer. The kind that chooses not to inspect important things on a pontoon boat, such as *the pontoons!* The kind of guy that sees the boat leaning slightly to the front right but doesn't think that will matter once you crank up the engine to full throttle!

Now picture this: six people, most of whom were over six feet in height, all sitting closely together, with all our coolers, chairs, and kids in the front part of a slightly forward-leaning pontoon boat. I slowly coasted out past the safety buoys, waiting patiently so I could slam down the throttle and hit mach speed; and once we went past the floating speed signs, that's exactly what I did.

When the lake started rapidly rushing over the bow of the boat, it became apparent that something was going wrong—and going wrong rather quickly!

The pontoon on the right side had acquired a leak over the winter and had taken in quite a bit of water. Then imagine all this weight sitting on the front. I was watching my twenty-six-foot-long boat go under at what seemed like a forty-five degree angle, quickly.

The good news was that as soon as I let off the throttle (which by the way was very quickly), the front of the boat came right back up on top of the surface. We hastily decided that all of our belongings and us would stay afloat better and dryer if we repositioned everything in the back half of the boat. It no longer took a rocket scientist to figure out the front of the boat wasn't a safe or smart place to ride, especially when half of Beaver Lake decided to come over the top of it.

Believe it or not, in spite of all that, it turned out to be a pleasant day with our friends. We were even able to take the boat out on the lake, albeit not too far and certainly not too fast!

This is the lesson that I learned from that experience: simply put, anything man-made is sinkable! Anything that man puts together, man can also tear apart; and if by chance a hole is found in the vessel (your family), then all it will take is a little speed in an out-of-balance life to exploit the hole and your boat will rapidly sink too.

I have no idea how that hole got there. It could have happened just by normal aging or wear and tear. It could have happened while bringing the boat back into dock the summer before, or it could have been hit by another vessel. The point is that there was a breach in the hull, and I simply refused to address the obvious issue. Instead of doing the right thing and examining the boat thoroughly and seeking any needed repairs, I simply looked the other way and almost had a disaster on my hands.

How familiar does that sound, dad? How many unattended issues are causing your family to slowly sink? How long will you simply turn your head and look the other way when you know or even just sense that something might be wrong? How much indifference and missed baseball games can you feed your son until it's engrained into him that he's just not a priority to you? How much neglect, inattention, and dereliction of duty will your daughter take from you until she looks for love elsewhere? If the constant gift you give your family is neglect, or the words you say to your children most often are "just a minute," then you're well on your way to the bottom of the lake.

Untended holes in the souls of fathers will ultimately lead to a life out of balance, and it definitely takes a balanced heart to become a successful father. How balanced are you, dad? Did you know that fathers intent on being the hard-nosed, non-loving, no-emotion, "my way or the highway" kind of dads are going to raise some extremely frustrated kids? Some men really think the old school is the best school and are just a lot more concerned about how strong they sound than how much love they give. Danger, dads! Because if that's you, then you're tipping way too far to one side; and before you know it, it's going to be too late!

On the other hand—and just as bad—are the fathers who never get involved. They never leave their comfort zone or their comfort chair. They never get connected, they never communicate, and they never show the love and compassion that is

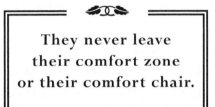

> They never leave their comfort zone or their comfort chair.

absolutely critical in order to raise confident children. They simply leave their responsibilities to another, and when you do that, dad, you simply open the door for destruction to enter your home.

Guess what, guys? It wasn't the iceberg's fault for sinking the *Titanic*. The iceberg wasn't mean or evil. It wasn't out stalking an innocent victim. It was just a natural phenomenon; frozen water that had broken off from its wall, freely floating in the North Atlantic. It wasn't the iceberg's fault; it was *Titanic* that failed. So too, it is our responsibility to keep our families on course and collision free.

The iceberg was neither good nor bad. By itself, it was neutral; it was the carelessness of the ship that caused the devastation. The iceberg can be a lot like marriage. The term "marriage" itself is neutral, yet it's what goes into it that determines its destiny. It is intended to be an incredible picture of two individuals uniting together to create a beautiful family. It obviously takes a committed man and woman to make it successful, but once again marriage is just the vehicle that houses the family. It's what kind of life we place into that vehicle that determines its destiny.

It's similar to parenting. The term "parenting" by itself is abstract, but it's the life and the action placed into it—and how that life grows and is nurtured—that determines its success.

The lesson is simple. Holes—and their subsequent damage in the hearts and souls of fathers—can lead to harm for the family, and the problem has to be quickly dealt with and repaired. If we don't fix it, life will exploit the breach, and destruction will come to the father and the child. We must address and fix the holes in our hearts. The stakes are simply too high!

There are times when you know things aren't quite right at home. Maybe you've been gone too much or working too late, and instead of stopping long enough to examine your family for some damage to its pontoons, you simply refuse to deal with the critical and important issues. You wake up one day and destruction is coming over the front of your boat; your home is rapidly sinking! We think our plan is sufficient, only to realize that the ocean of life can be so overwhelming that it constantly exploits all of the holes in our hearts. And all of it could have been avoided, but this is the twenty-first century, and it's too much of a hassle to take the time for a little self-examination. By the time the holes are found, dad, the alarms have already sounded and destructive collision is in clear view.

If this is what's happening to you, then you need to do the same thing I did years ago as I watched my boat sink. I pulled back on the throttle and stopped the boat, and it quickly came back up above the surface. You see, it could still float. It just couldn't go at any great speed with that much weight placed in it. Once we realized what the problem was, we shifted the weight more evenly and took back off again, albeit at a much slower speed.

That's what needs to happen to families all across this world. Men need to pull back on the throttle and stop the boat. You need to stop the incredible pace that we all find ourselves in and take the time, however long it takes, to redistribute the weight in your home. Out-of-balance men and out-of-balance families, if left unrepaired, will ultimately sink, and you had better pull back on the throttle now before that becomes your fate.

It might be just the time to get away from your job, or the neighborhood or anything that weighs down your home and just get away for some rethinking and rebuilding of your family. Go camping. Go to the beach. Go somewhere where you and your household can clear the air, and start on your journey again. And leave your business behind! Jobs can change and so can a career, but a family is meant for a lifetime.

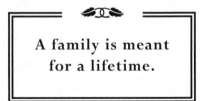

A family is meant
for a lifetime.

That weekend at the lake I found out that it takes a lot more than just good plans and wishes to make an excellent family weekend, and I'm telling you now that it's going to take a lot more than wishful thinking to make a family succeed. And you will need to make any necessary repairs to your "boat" before you take it out again, regardless of the cost.

Did you know that the *Titanic* cost over seven million dollars to build back then? Its hull weighed approximately 26,000 tons, and the ship itself weighed in at over 46,000 gross tons. It had nine decks, which made it stand as high as an eleven-story building. Each funnel was large enough for a train to drive through, and its anchors weighed approximately thirty-one tons. Each link in an anchor chain weighed 175 pounds. The *Titanic* was divided by fifteen bulkheads, because when it was extended above the water line, the ship was thought to be watertight—meaning that if even some of its compartments were filled with ocean water, she could still remain afloat!

Do you get the picture? It was designed to last. It was constructed so mightily that no one would have ever thought that its life span would be so short. But it was!

Men, listen. Nothing man-made is unsinkable. All the meticulous work that went into making *Titanic*, all the checking, double checking, and triple checking, and all the failsafe plans that were made, failed. It came down to something as small and simple as a missing pair of binoculars—the eyes of the ship. That's us, dads!

All the gifts, toys, and unfulfilled promises add up to a total that lacks what it takes for your family to be successful. That will only come when our eyes are focused in the right direction. Making plans is only part of the formula that will provide success for you and your family. The other half of the equation is achievement. It's actually doing whatever it takes to get the job done.

Are there holes in your home? You had better take the time to examine your ship and immediately make any needed repairs. Being out of balance is destructive, and eventually it will expose any holes in your hull. Pull back on the throttle, dads, and if by some

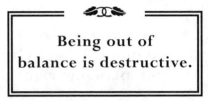

Being out of balance is destructive.

chance you're still not convinced that you need to do this, then all I can say is that you had better don the life jackets!

ACTION POINTS

1. How long has it been since you told your child you love him or her? If it's been more than a few minutes, do it again!

2. Have you put your job second this week in favor of an activity with your family? If not, plan one right now.

3. When was the last time you had a "date" with your wife? Call the babysitter and set a date for the two of you to rediscover your passion—and make those plans today!

4. When was the last time you got alone by yourself and carefully examined your heart and the state of your home? If it's been over one month since you've done so, sit down tonight after everyone has gone to bed and begin the process! Write down your thoughts and the changes you want to make in your home, and then share those positive action steps with your family the next day.

5. Are you already aware of some repairs that need to be made to your soul or to the soul of someone in your family? Why begin tomorrow, begin right now.

CHAPTER FIVE

THEY PAID LITTLE ATTENTION
TO THE WARNING SIGNS

Some time ago, our family decided to take a trip to the Smokey Mountains of North Carolina during our kids' spring break from school. The five of us loaded up in our van, making our journey across the southeastern part of the U.S. on our way to a time of rest and family time. As we were cruising across a major interstate, we passed through a large amount of construction, and at one point we came across a sign warning that traffic could slow down or even come to a stop because of the roadwork. So the need to be cautious was apparent. It was obvious that our travel time was going to be extended, because traffic would come to a complete stop and the line of cars and trucks seemed to stretch for miles.

The second time we had come to this interstate traffic jam, we were completely stopped in the left-hand lane. As we were just sitting there waiting for traffic to begin moving again, I noticed that just a few car lengths ahead of us was a school bus stopped in the right hand lane. We were just talking and waiting to move again when all of a sudden a horrible image flashed before our eyes. An SUV towing some sort of trailer came flying into our peripheral vision. It was very obvious that the driver had failed to heed the warning signs, and because of that neglect there was going to be a terrible crash!

It was happening all too fast, yet somehow eerily seemed to be occurring in slow motion. The driver had obviously locked up his brakes, but there was just too much weight and too little distance. It was just impossible to stop it in time.

It is a terrible thing to be driving along and come up on a wreck that has just occurred, but it is greatly magnified when you watch one actually happen! And if this scenario could get any worse, it was apparent that the school bus was directly in the path of this out-of-control vehicle. We could easily see this wreck rapidly unfolding, and my wife cried out that it was going to slam into the bus. And it did.

Words cannot describe the sight of this horrendous crash and the feeling that came with it. The trailer they were towing just exploded and clothes and belongings went everywhere. Glass shattered and metal was crushed. It was simply horrible.

It is at this point that any previous training in first aid or anything else like that just seems to leave you as you sink into a mental and emotional funk because of what you have just witnessed. I handed my cell phone to Liz and told her to call 911 to get someone out there quickly. I then turned around and told our children, all of who had witnessed the wreck and were obviously shaken, to turn their heads and not look at what might be a gruesome scene.

I knew that I needed to get over there as quickly as possible, but yet at the same time I knew part of me really didn't want to go over to the site because of what I might find. I got out of the van and begin to head toward the crash. The trailer had slammed into the bus with such an incredible force that it just seemed to explode on impact, while the back of the bus was literally crushed to where the back right seat was smashed up against the next to last seat. Several people began to arrive at the wreck and began to examine all those involved. Another passerby and I began to examine the bus to see if there were any children in it.

Now here is where the miracles begin to unfold. First of all, there were no children on the bus, which was lifesaving in and of itself, because if there would have been kids present, there would most certainly have been a horrible tragedy. Second, the entire family that was in the SUV was unharmed and was just trying to regain their composure from their terrible crash. The only person injured was the driver of the bus, who, after about fifteen minutes or so after the wreck, began to have slight stiffening in her neck from the unexpected crash. It was an absolute miracle that there were no serious injuries, much less fatalities! No question about it—a miracle.

When it was all done, I got back into the van to continue our vacation. You know how it is when you're almost in an accident and after a few seconds your adrenaline has worn off and you get this sudden feeling that just makes your legs turn to noodles? That's what began to happen to me, and for miles all I could think about was replaying that crash scene over and over in my mind, and I couldn't help but think about what would have happened should there have been kids riding on the bus—especially in the back row. I kept thinking of innocent children, who wouldn't be thinking about anything of this nature; kids just going through life laughing and playing games when all of a sudden, someone who didn't heed the warning signs lost control and brought sudden destruction upon innocent children's lives. That vision just wouldn't leave.

Tragically, a similar scenario is happening in families today. Dads who should be watching over their families and paying attention to the journey are turning their heads for a few moments at a critical time, and before they know it they're flying down life's highway completely out of control with a devastating collision staring straight at them. And try as they might, no matter how hard they push those brake pedals, it seems there's just too much weight and too little distance to stop in time.

Has it happened to you? And just as importantly, are we as dads really paying attention to how we steer our family on their life's course?

It was on the heels of another tragedy that the thought came to me that something needs to happen in our school system so concerned parents can become involved to make a positive difference in the lives of kids. As you can imagine, there are probably countless educational programs out there geared toward making a difference in a child's life, but the problem with some of them is that they treat the symptom and simply cover over the pain and do not cure the problem. Positive, lasting change seldom really takes place. So I began to think about what was missing in our schools, which, if present, could be used in a positive way to reach out to kids to try to prevent tragedies from happening.

I began to think about today's educational system, especially in our own children's school, and I thought about what was good in school and what wasn't and about who was there and who wasn't. And then the thought rang out so loudly that it became crystal clear—one of the major problems, if not the major problem, facing schools in America today. Where are the *fathers*? Where have they been, and where did they go?

You can talk all day long about the lack of funds that many schools face, the lack of discipline, or the lack of qualified teachers or teacher pay. But if you want to get to the root of the problem, then we need to get outside the schools and get inside the *home*.

Where did the fathers go? I'll tell you where we went. We checked out! We quit! We abandoned our ship. We've been at some place other than our post, and because of that choice, families are suffering needlessly because fathers

**We quit!
We abandoned
our ship.**

have found other things to capture their attention while their ship rapidly cruises toward disaster—unwatched, unprotected, and unloved.

Somewhere along the line, men have bought into a lie that says we will be the breadwinners (maybe) and moms will take care of raising the kids. This course has gone unchecked for so long and has been passed along through far too many generations with far too few stepping in to say enough is enough is

Better careers could replace beautiful children.

enough! Somewhere in the past, men decided that it was okay to become neglectful in our fathering duties and that better careers could replace beautiful children, and the need to have a bigger house became more important that the healing of a broken heart.

Yet this trap is very subtle. It's as though you have this beautiful yard that you have gone to great lengths and expense to plant. You map it out, buy the sod, and put the irrigation system in. And then you sit back to admire your work. However, instead of maintaining your yard, you then forget about it.

Maybe it's your golf game. Maybe it's the TV (we used to call it the idiot box at our house when I was growing up). Maybe it's your new job or the person next door. Whatever it is, it has turned your head from your priority, and now because of your negligence weeds have come up and choked out your grass so much that even the good seed you plant and sod you lay down doesn't make a difference. You can't even notice it because of the overabundance of weeds that now control what was once a beautiful lawn.

And do you know what? Those weeds just blew in from someone else's neglected yard. And those weeds blew in from their neighbor's yard. And you begin to trace out where all the weeds are coming from, and you find that some confused soul has nothing but weeds in his yard. I mean he's got no grass, no flowers, no shrubs, no nothing—just weeds. It's offensive and repulsive.

He has nothing but weeds in his yard because that's what his yard was like when he was growing up. It's because that was how his father showed him how to have a yard. And his father did it that way because his father's father did it that way. This is how generational mistakes are passed down until someone says, "That's not how you grow a lawn!"

The real tragedy, though, is that *you* let someone else's foolishness and senselessness affect your own house. These beliefs aren't your own, but you allowed yourself to be taken in by those devices—because you turned your head for one moment. You simply took your eyes off your priorities for a moment, and

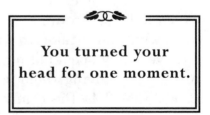

You turned your head for one moment.

suddenly the weeds came in and took control. You wake up one day and things are in such a mess at your house that there seems to be no hope and it's at this point that an outward manifestation of an inward neglect brings a destructive harvest.

The *Titanic* now rests beneath thousands of feet of water for several reasons, and one of the biggest ones is that those who directed the ship simply didn't stop long enough and pay attention to the warning signs. Don't forget, there were at least six warnings from other ships that had witnessed icebergs. Six times they received messages of caution, and six times those in charge failed to take those warnings seriously enough to prevent disaster.

Dads, where are we today? How many warning signs have we failed to heed from others who have experienced destruction? How do we stack up when it comes time to listening to our family? Is it a burden or a blessing to stop, listen, and find out what's going on with your family? Is it a pain or a pleasure to change our plans from what we desire to do to what we need to do to prove our commitment? And is it like pulling teeth to spend quality time with them?

We are the only ones who can truthfully answer those questions, but wherever you are on your path of fatherhood, this is a trustworthy yet sometimes painful way to see how we are measuring up to our responsibilities. We have to ask ourselves the tough questions. Are we paying close attention to those we've been called to lead? Are we making the necessary *sacrifices* to do whatever it takes to ensure success in our family? Are we really speaking blessings into our families, or are we just giving them some lip service in order to pacify them? Is there anything that is more important—such as a job, career, sports, people, TV, or anything else at all—and takes precedence over our top priority, our family?

How does your "yard" look, dad? Are you keeping your eyes on the road? If not, then it is up to you to make those necessary changes in order to make sure you're doing your job when it comes to leading your family. Near misses and nearly fatal (and fatal) crashes to our homes don't have to happen if we as men are watching over our family. Are you paying attention to the signs? Do you even know they are there? Stay alert, dad, because much is at stake.

ACTION POINTS

1. When was the last time you sat down with each of your children individually to see how they're doing? Sit down with at least one of them before the end of the day and see if they are happy or if there is some uneasiness within them. If you can't tell the difference, you know you need to immediately begin to spend more time with them.

2. Have you checked out your kids' life at school? Have you visited them at school just to show them you love them? Surprise them at school; or better yet, if possible and permissible, check them out for a lunch with daddy!

3. Have other things captured your attention such as recreation or work? If so, startle your family with a surprise weekend getaway or at least determine to fast from your favorite recreation time this weekend in order to spend time with your family.

4. Are you closely watching your children and the friendships they develop? Are they forming relationships that you know aren't healthy? If so, take appropriate action quickly, such as beginning to make your home a more enjoyable place to be. Show them you care by effectively communicating to them and by sincerely listening to them.

CHAPTER SIX

HOW YOU DRIVE THE SHIP DETERMINES HOW YOU WILL FINISH THE JOURNEY!

A few years ago, my wife and I were out of town, staying with some friends. On Sunday night of our trip, our host invited us to go with him and took us to a detention facility for troubled youth. He had volunteered to work with young people who made some bad choices and had gotten themselves into serious trouble—typically with some sort of substance abuse—and this type of facility was their last chance to get cleaned up or things would get even worse. His mission was simply to go in, to listen, and to share with these troubled teens that there really was an answer to their problems other than the self-destructive path they had chosen. Since our work is to go into schools and to get dads and kids to reconnect to one another, I thought this might be really helpful and informative, but little did I know what I was about to see and hear.

Never having been to a facility like this, I really didn't know what to expect. As volunteers, we were taken to a cafeteria and told to wait for the kids to be sent in. As we waited, I tried to imagine what they would look like. Would they have spiked hair, twenty-two earrings, and tattoos all over? What was their demeanor going to be like? Would they be bitter, hateful, resentful, and ungrateful?

I was really surprised when the doors opened up and the young people were ushered in. Six beautiful, innocent-looking teens. They were the all-American kids next door. There were two boys and four girls, and each one had a different, tragic story. Five of the six were talkative, and for the most part were really outgoing. The sixth was a young man who quietly sat next to me. You could literally see the hurt and pain that was overflowing from his heart and had found its way to his countenance. After a few minutes of talking, my friend turned the conversation to me, and since we work with kids and fathers and their relationship to each other, I thought it would be helpful to find out where each of them stood in their relationship to their dads. I wasn't prepared to find out what I was about to hear. I simply asked them to tell me about their relationship to their dads, and serious pain began to pour out of everyone who spoke!

The first one spoke up, a sweet little sixteen-year-old girl. She said, "My father left me when I was eleven. No note, no words, no call, no nothing. When my father left me, I was playing with dolls, but within a year I was trying to cut myself and then later I tried to take my life." And then I heard something that is far too common among abandoned children. She said, "I didn't know what I did to make him leave. Was it my fault?" Thus she began a downward spiral that led to a destructive path of abusing her mind and then her body. She finished her sad testimony by telling us to tell dads not to leave their homes and families.

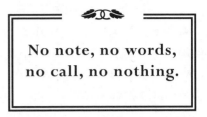

No note, no words, no call, no nothing.

Are you listening, dad? Now think about what she said: the obvious turning point in her life came when her father checked out.

The next young person spoke up. A handsome sixteen- or seventeen-year-old young man whose first words out of his mouth were, "My dad's an alcoholic." He went on to say that his mom was the spiritual leader of their family.

Then the quiet young man sitting next to me spoke up and began to tell a tragic story of how his father was killed when he was young; and that he never got the chance to know his dad. He told of how his stepfather is neglectful in his fathering duties to his younger brother.

Later he came up to me after our time with them was over and shared his appreciation to us for taking time to bring some encouragement to him. He went on to share with us that his mother had told him that his father grew up in a home where his own father wasn't much of a dad and thus was simply passing on what he learned from his own father. I shared with him that he had to determine to break this destructive cycle passed on from one generation to the next and decide that he would never carry that to his future wife and children.

The next one spoke up, a precious teenage girl who said that several months ago her father put his hands on her in an inappropriate way, and now there were charges against him. The last to speak was a teenage girl who began to tell how she was the product of divorce and that her stepfather showed favoritism to his biological children over his new ones.

Six teenagers, all in trouble. Five of them spoke out about the lack of connection with their fathers, all sharing a common denominator—a dysfunctional relationship with dad.

I realize this case study is somewhat anecdotal, and most researchers might scoff at such a small number of participants, but that night we all walked away from that place knowing we had just met teenagers in serious trouble. These were mere children who had really messed up their lives and who would face serious consequences unless they were able to turn it around. Yet almost all of them were courageous enough to speak out about this all too common affliction called "fatherlessness."

It's how you drive the ship, dad, that determines how you'll reach your destination. Think about the night of April 14, 1912. When the *Titanic* struck the iceberg, it was traveling around top speed—somewhere around twenty-two knots—and it was at night. She was in an iceberg field, and they *knew* it! They'd had sufficient warnings but it was still ill-equipped and unprepared for the task of avoiding a collision. Those in charge failed to change their direction or their speed, despite the danger.

Dads, where are we? How are we driving our own ship? How are we handling the task of fathering? There is a universal law that will never be broken: you reap what you sow. To the *Titanic*, it meant that they couldn't take that route at that time of night at that speed without a disaster. To a sports team it simply means you can't consistently practice with a mediocre and nonchalant work ethic and expect to turn it up on game day and win. To a business it means you cannot lag behind your competition in morale, innovative ideas, creative thinking, and modern technology and expect to keep

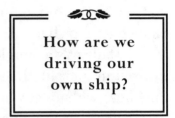

How are we driving our own ship?

your market share. To a nation, it means you can't progress unless you value life, freedom, and respect for others. And for families—and especially fathers—it clearly means you cannot plant seeds of inattention, abandonment, and neglect in your home and expect to reap a harvest of a successful family. It won't happen because it can't happen.

Here's an interesting thought to consider: What are you planting in your children's lives? What kind of future are you putting out before them? Did you know that we live in a nation where almost forty percent of the children will go to bed tonight in a home without their natural father and around twenty-five percent of them will go to bed tonight without *any* father figure in the home? Startling statistics aren't they?

I sometimes wonder whatever happened to those young people that I met that Sunday night. Unless a miracle occurs, I'll probably never know; but I just hope what little time we had with them spoke life into them and planted some seeds of love and acceptance.

On that Sunday night in 1912, those lost souls who found themselves in the dark waters in the North Atlantic never had a real chance of survival, and tragically many kids who find themselves in the dark waters in this mixed-up world never have much of a chance for survival either. So what are we going to do?

Dads, it's a simple truth, but many never learn to grasp it in their lifetime. What we do and what we say—and how we say it—lays the foundation for our children's lives. Don't let your decisions for your family mirror the decisions of those in charge of the *Titanic*, recklessly charging ahead into dangerous waters.

How are you driving your ship? The future of those on board depends on you.

ACTION POINTS

1. Do you ever show any favoritism to any one child? Or perhaps more likely, do you have a child with whom you aren't as well connected as the others? If so, make a special point of spending some time with him or her today!

2. How do you think your children describe you or their relationship with you to others when you're not around? Ask them sometime.

3. Do you need a little help sometimes? Do you have an unhealthy habit that might be affecting your children's lives? If you have addictions or other issues you can't seem to conquer alone, seek out professionals, or friends you can really trust, or a good church and begin making a difference in yourself so you can make a difference for your kids!

CHAPTER SEVEN

WRONG PRIORITIES WILL
LEAD TO A SHIPWRECK

It was another Sunday night but not *just* any other Sunday night. This was the night that my favorite professional football team was going to play their archrivals on national television—prime time! It was a big-time game, and I was in a big-time mood to watch this event. So like most red-blooded American males who want to watch football, I found my favorite couch and proceeded to do the normal thing, which was to become totally oblivious to the world around me—or as my wife so eloquently puts it, I went into my "blue funk." You know what I'm talking about don't you, guys? This state of funk or mental and emotional oblivion is hard work and takes great concentration, because how else can you explain how any human being can drown out screaming kids, telephone rings, people knocking at the door, and your wife trying to communicate with you unless you have a master's degree in shutting out the world?

This night was destined to be different because our youngest daughter, Madison, took it upon herself to try to get daddy to come back down to earth, get his head out of the television, and do something so ridiculous as turning off the game and playing with his baby daughter. Now as I write this, I find it extremely difficult to figure out why I would have such difficulty spending time with someone I love so much. After all, it was just a football game.

But that night, I walked into a snare that too many men step into and many times never break loose of until it is too late. That night, I wanted to choose football over family. My priority had drifted from things of extreme importance that I could participate in and make a lasting impact on to something in which I was only a spectator

> My priority had drifted.

and the outcome of which I didn't have any influence. I found myself cheering for those who don't even know me—and certainly couldn't hear me—and I found myself neglecting those who covet time with me and who long to speak to me.

To make a long explanation short, I blew it.

Madison wanted to go outside. I wanted to stay inside. She wanted time with daddy, and I wanted time with Dallas. Guess who won? At first, she was somewhat content just to let me run after her outside in the front yard and then let me go in and catch up on what had transpired for the past few plays. But it was getting down to crunch time. The fourth quarter was just beginning, and surely I could make even a four-year-old comprehend the significance of the moment. But I couldn't. And to confuse matters even more, she determined that since she was having a great time having daddy chase her around the yard, she began to refuse to allow me time to go in and have a two-

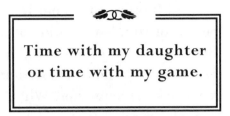

Time with my daughter or time with my game.

or-three minute rest, which obviously I was using to catch up on the current status of the game. It came down to a matter of choice—time with my daughter or time with my game.

I knew that if I chose time with Madison, I would surely miss an important play that could determine the outcome of the game. The real irony here is that every day we have opportunities to leave a lasting positive impression on our children that will help determine *their* outcome. What to do? I even tried to play with her while the team was in the huddle and then race back into the house to catch the next play and then run back out into the yard for fifteen seconds of quality time with her.

But that wasn't going to work, and we both knew it. Madison or football; football or Madison. I thought long and hard and then made what I felt was an earth-shattering, Noble-Prize-like decision—I sent out our seven-year-old daughter to take my place and fill the gap. Well, that went over like a lead balloon, and I looked out the front door to see my four-year-old standing there crying for me—and I don't just mean a sniffle and a play tear. I'm talking about the real thing. I saw a four-year-old crying real tears and letting out a loud wail as she watched her daddy find his enjoyment in *things* rather than her.

I finally coaxed her into coming inside for a short period of time so I could continue to watch the game. But still she wanted my full attention, so she sat down beside me on the couch and attempted to get me to at least acknowledge her. When she didn't get the attention she needed (not just desired), she simply walked over to another chair and just sat down.

What happened next was kind of just a blur. My wife had moved the club chair Madison was sitting in to the edge of the kitchen floor because we were going to have the carpets cleaned the next day, so the chair straddled the carpeted floor of the living room and the tile floor of the kitchen. Madison wanted to get out of the chair then, but somehow when she scooted out to get down she lost her balance and fell headfirst toward the floor and I heard a slapping sound—the kind of slap that happens when you smack your open hand on the tile floor. I thought that's what it was, but it wasn't.

Instead of it being her hand slapping on the tile floor, it was both bones in her left arm snapping *in two* as she tried to brace herself from the fall! After hearing that awful sound, my wife came running in from around the corner about the same time I also got to Madison. As we lifted the sleeve of her new shirt, it was very apparent that her arm was badly broken (a doctor friend of ours who saw her in the emergency room commented that it was about the worst deformity that he had seen on an arm).

The next four hours were pretty much a blur, also, as Madison went from having an IV to X-rays to the *operating room* to get her arm set. We got home after ten o'clock that night.

Not surprisingly, the outcome of the football game meant nothing to me anymore. My main goal was how we were going to administer a healing touch to her and to make the next few weeks easier for a four-year-old who still wasn't quite sure what had happened to her.

Early the next morning as I was reflecting on what had transpired, I began a very painful evaluation of my priorities—or lack thereof—and it became very apparent to me there was a reason we had spent four hours in the emergency room and a lot of money that day. Most important of all, I realized my role in having caused great pain to my daughter and our family was a direct result of my neglect.

Did you get that, dads? *My* neglect; not someone else's—mine. You see, if I had been willing to sacrifice some of my leisure time by breaking away from a *game* (which had absolutely no relevance to my child's current need and future destiny), then I would have been outside with her all along. She never would have sat in a chair across the room, rejected by her dad. She would not have fallen and broken her arm.

Now, you might be saying, "Wait a minute! Come on, Moore. You really don't expect me to buy that, do you? Surely you don't really expect me to believe that just because you chose not to play with your daughter she broke her arm?"

Without question, yes I do. In those early morning hours, it became extremely clear to me that had I been willing to participate in quality time strengthening my relationship with my daughter and building her soul, I would not have had to spend a painful time in a hospital room watching a doctor rebuild my baby's arm.

Now, let me take a little time to paint the big picture on what happened. My daughter's injury came about from a fall that didn't have to happen. But I want to make it **extremely clear** that not *all* injuries or tragedies come from dad's or mom's neglect. This is a dark world, and unfair things happen to different people every day. Far too often innocent kids get sick, hurt, or leave this world much too early. This certainly **doesn't mean** it was the parent's fault. Please understand that! Comparing the two concepts would be like comparing apples to alligators! The two just don't mesh.

But what I want to clearly and emphatically communicate to everyone, especially fathers, is that it doesn't matter if it's your four-year-old daughter or your twenty-four-year-old son, children need, desire, long for, and cry out for your attention, your acceptance, your approval, and your blessing. They will pretty much go to any lengths to receive it, and if we as parents can learn this early enough, then we can possibly avoid many pitfalls that often hurt families.

Now, there is no way we can be with our children twenty-four hours a day, seven days a week. But here is what we can do—we can let them know from the very beginning of their lives that we are here for them and that we are willing to do everything we need to do to shape them and mold them into becoming the exact person they were created to be. And if we can prove this to them when they are young, then we can have more confidence that they may not fall into some of the snares and traps that kids who suffer because of neglect fall into.

The older they get, the larger and more dangerous the snares become. For example, my neglect showed my daughter that she had to go somewhere else to find her enjoyment, and a broken arm was the result. But what happens when it's a sixteen-year-old boy and he harvests the seeds of inattention and neglect you've planted? I guarantee it can be far worse than broken bones.

Studies show that when fathers are not a positive part of their children's lives—or have quality interaction with them—those children are at a higher risk of having a troubled life including poverty, drug and alcohol abuse, poor physical and emotional health, educational underachievement, crime, and teen pregnancy.

During my first draft of writing this book, I included a lot of studies at this part of the chapter to verify my beliefs, but I have taken them out for two reasons. First, I don't need a bunch of academic proof for reinforcing my beliefs about my own children; and second, we as fathers don't need to take a lot of time reading a bunch of studies. Instead, we should use that time to get connected with our children instead of just reading about the consequences of not being connected.

I don't think I've ever met a single person who has said to me, "Wow, I read these statistics on fathering, and they really changed my life." But I do meet many dads who, when they taste the blessings of what fathering can be or when they have experienced their own shipwreck, desire a change.

Dads, there is a direct correlation between the destiny of our children and the amount of attention, care, nurture, leadership, and love we give them. It's time that we wake up to this fact and begin to do something about it. Wouldn't it be incredible if children everywhere had the blessing and approval of their fathers, which would help them to never look for it in other people and in other things?

In the book of Proverbs, it says that the tongue has the power of life and death. Tonight children all across this nation and world will go to bed crying out to hear words like, "Son, I love you," or, "Sweetie, I'm proud of you, keep up the great work!" Dads, these words are words of *life* that are incredible, life-changing, and are desperately needed in order for your child to grow up confident of your love and commitment to them. They keep them from looking for attention elsewhere! But tragically, many kids will

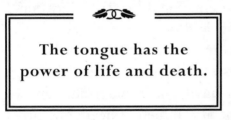

The tongue has the power of life and death.

never hear words similar to those—much less experience the blessings they bring. They will never hear them as long as we fathers are focused on things that are unimportant and irrelevant to the success of our children.

So, dads, once again the choice is ours. We can learn early on that children are going to look to us for attention, acceptance, and approval. We can learn early that if they don't find it in us it will be easier for them to fall prey to many of the dark snares that lure innocent children from their intended destiny.

Fathers that don't stand for something will raise children that can fall for anything.

You know, guys, it sure seems that on that Sunday night the men in charge of the ship were not focused on their priorities, and a devastating wreck occurred. Sunday nights are best when we spend them at home with family and not in the icy waters of the North Atlantic.

There were many things I learned the night my daughter broke her arm, but the two biggest ones were these: first of all, it *is* possible for a father to be there physically but not there emotionally. And second, it's much better to be a father that builds a soul than one who watches a doctor rebuild broken bones—and it doesn't matter if it is a broken arm or a broken heart, fathers must begin to realize that it is much easier to build a child's character than it is to repair a broken life.

1. Do sporting events or anything else on TV take precedence over your family? If so, then shock your family by turning off the TV and making it into a family day or evening!

2. Next time you do something with your family, make sure your heart and attention are totally there and that you're not just taking up space.

3. Have you used one of your vacation days lately to surprise your family and take them on a picnic or some other outing? If not, make plans today!

4. Are you giving your children any reasons to look for love and affection elsewhere? Before you put them to bed tonight, make sure to let them know you love them.

CHAPTER EIGHT

STICKS AND STONES CAN BREAK MY BONES BUT WORDS— THEY'RE A REAL KILLER

We've all heard the saying, "Sticks and stones may break my bones, but words can never hurt me!" It sounds great, doesn't it? It sounds so noble and all-American. The problem is that it's so radically far from truth. It's stupid in its premise, and it's illogical in its content. Anyone who believes this, is sadly mistaken and has probably wounded many hearts. Saying words don't hurt makes as much sense as playing with fire and expecting not to get burned.

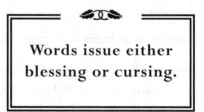

Words issue either blessing or cursing.

Words issue either blessing or cursing, and your life is often a direct result of the verbal seeds that were sown into it. In other words, what and how we speak to others can either be an encouragement or a detriment. We'll either build others up or bring them down with our words.

The night of *Titanic's* disaster, the radio operator received a very important message from the *Californian* warning them of impending danger. Do you remember how the message was received and what the reply was from *Titanic*? "Keep out! Shut up! I am busy . . ."

The real tragedy was that *Titanic's* radio operator got his wish. He was doing his job, but in the midst of all the hard work he must have been doing that night, a voice was loudly calling out to him—a voice of legitimate warning that he did not heed. Not only did it fall on deaf ears, it received a sharp and cutting response. "Keep out! Shut up! I am busy . . ."

In other words, he was saying, "Stay out of my space, leave me alone, and don't bother me now. What you have to say isn't important to me!" As fathers, we have all had words come out of our mouths that were spoken harshly and without any forethought.

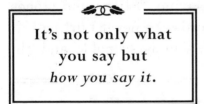

It's not only what you say but *how you say it.*

We have shot back replies just like this radio operator's, answers that have pierced and wounded our family members, and we have seen the looks of discouragement and disbelief with which our family members receive our words.

It's sickening to think how many times damaging seeds are planted by fathers who, in the heat of the moment, fail to realize that in the eyes of a child it's not only what you say but *how you say it* that solidifies how you feel about them.

What is it that makes our words so powerful? Why is it that it only takes a few misguided and misdirected statements to damage or even destroy a soul? They're only sounds coming from our mouths—phonics mixed with a few vowels. Can they really be that powerful, or are we just making a big deal out of nothing?

The answer is of course something we already know—they can be used to promote life, or they can be an instrument of destruction and death. And the most disturbing thing about them is that they are simply the manifestation of our hearts.

Extract juice from a fresh apple and you get great-tasting apple juice; squeeze juice from a rattlesnake and you get poisonous venom that destroys and sometimes even kills. Perhaps one reason words can be so damaging is that sometimes when we speak hastily, unfiltered from our hearts, those hearing them might realize those words are a representation of the heart.

Now listen, I'm not saying that just because you answer in a frustrated way that you hate your child. There are times when the pressures of life sometimes push out an ugly response, but just try and explain your response to a six-year-old or a sixteen-year-old; the water can get pretty muddy as you try to explain yourself. It would be like hitting someone in the face and immediately trying to take away the pain. You just can't do that!

Dads, what kind of words are we speaking *into* our children? Are they words that promote healing or words that hurt and discourage? What type of response do your kids expect from you on a regular basis? Have you instilled confidence in your family so that everyone knows they can come to you anytime, anywhere and know that they will get the time, attention, and gracious response they need? Or have you cultivated intimated and scared kids that are confused much of the time about when and where it's appropriate to communicate with you, hoping they caught you in the right mood?

Think about your time with your family and about the type of communication you presently have with your kids. How frequent is it? How serious is it? Is it just surface stuff, or is it about things that are important to the hearts of your children? Are they asking you for the keys to their lives, or are they just asking you for the keys to your car? Does your child come to you with questions about school, relationships, problems, and silly stuff? Do they come to you at work? Do they come to you after work? Do they come to you at all? As fathers, we've got to quickly learn that our kids will consistently go to those who they think will listen to them and who will care—or at least act like they care—about what they have to say. Dangerous and deadly relationships are formed every day as a result of fathers not having a tender heart and a listening ear for their child, because then they just might turn to someone else.

Dads, we've got to learn this now. We've got to plant this into our being so deep that it will never be uprooted. Children have an incredible need for acceptance from their fathers, and many times they will listen, follow, and obey those dads who prove their love and concern to them. But know this as well:

children whose fathers are too busy, too distant, and too enamored with things that are only temporary will invariably go to other sources to find that love and acceptance.

Little girls whose father hasn't taken the time to cultivate a deep and lasting relationship with them often find seeds of promiscuity planted in their lives because of their father's inattention. If the daughter doesn't have a father who fills her needs for security, that act of neglect on the father's part can open the door for her to find it elsewhere.

Come on, dads—for a gender who prides itself on conquering the foe and claiming the prize, we seem to become flagrant cowards when it comes time to raising our daughters. Let's not fall back on some faint and chickenhearted excuse that we think will allow us to excuse ourselves from our responsibility of pointing our daughters on a protected and pure path. It *is* our responsibility, and we had better learn it now before someone else is forced to try to fill our shoes.

Most men seemingly need to have a problem right in our face before we deal with it or believe it even exists. If we don't take the time to effectively communicate our daughters' value to us, someone else will. And if we don't get our feet off the golf course or our faces out of the TV to show proper love, acceptance, and affection to them, then someone else will. And I can promise you that whoever substitutes for us will likely not be able to supply to her the guidance toward her destiny that God intended we provide.

Please, dads, wherever you may be with your children right now, begin to learn that words cultivate life or create loneliness. They can start wars or promote peace. They can cause hearts to harden or wounds to heal. They can cause kids to love or to leave, and they can cause faults to be repeated or revive families. Over time, what you say may be forgotten, but the way you say it *will not*.

One last thing about this issue of words: What do you think the radio operator of the *Titanic* thought when the message came to him from his superiors that the ship was going down? Were those warnings he tossed aside important now?

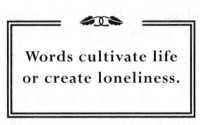

Words cultivate life or create loneliness.

Dads, when you get the news about some tragedy in your home, it is often too late. The radio operator could type "SOS" as fast as humanly possible, but it wasn't going to save the ship now.

What are we saying, and how are we saying it? What type of words leave our lips, dads? Sticks and stones—yeah, they hurt a lot, but a killer tongue can last a lifetime. What type of words leave our lips, dads? Our children's lives are hanging in the balance. The choice is ours.

Action Points

1. When was the last time you looked your child in the eye and told him or her you were sorry for what you said and how you said it? It doesn't matter how long ago the offense might have taken place; before the end of the day, make sure you've tried to make it right.

2. Have you called your older children lately with nothing else to say to them except the words, "I love you?" If not, do it right now!

3. Have you told your wife that you love her today? If not, stop reading right now and say it to her!

4. Are you sensitive to your daughter and her feelings? Have you realized she might need a little extra attention from you, dad? Maybe a long walk and a long talk with your daughter might be the answer—plan one today!

CHAPTER NINE

WHAT WAS SUPPOSED TO SAVE IT ACTUALLY SANK IT

When *Titanic* struck the iceberg, the ship immediately began to sink—and quickly at that. What was supposed to be the unsinkable became the unthinkable, and not only was it going down to the bottom of the ocean, it was doing so at an alarming rate.

Now think about this: we have talked about how untouchable so many people said the *Titanic* was; but have you ever been told why it was thought to have been so impervious? I've told you that many people said it was unsinkable, but do you know why they said that?

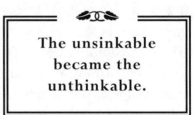

The unsinkable became the unthinkable.

One of the reasons it was given that title was because of the engineering of its lower interior. The *Titanic* was designed with huge walls in its hull that, when closed, formed watertight compartments. These transverse bulkheads, as they were called, were designed so that each compartment could be immediately sealed off, thereby containing any water that entered because of some type of damage. This was to keep it from traveling to another compartment in the hull. Sounds great, doesn't it? It makes sense even to people who know little about naval construction—such as myself.

There was one little problem: these bulkheads could only be shut off horizontally, not vertically!

Shortly after the collision when the crew recognized there was damage to some of those compartments, they were immediately shut off; but remember, they could only be closed from side to side, not top to bottom. Add to this that the top of each wall was barely above the waterline of the ship; therefore, when ocean water began to flood the compartments that were damaged, it soon began to spill over the top of these bulkheads and into the adjacent compartments.

Do you get the picture? The ocean water pouring in had nowhere to go once each airtight compartment filled—except over the top of the wall and into the next compartment. This in turn caused the front of this huge ship to pitch and be pushed further and further underwater, which only exacerbated the problem. And all the while, more and more water flooded into the damaged compartments, one after the other, pulling the ship further down at a faster rate.

The tragic irony was this: the very thing that was supposed to make this dream ship unsinkable turned out to be the catalyst for a nightmare. What was thought to be the answer actually became part of the problem, and here is the lesson that we as fathers can learn from this tragedy. Flawed engineering left unchecked and unchanged will ultimately lead to disaster. On paper those transverse bulkheads looked like the real deal, but in the real world they proved not only to be useless but also became the guarantee for disaster.

The life-saver in reality became a life-taker. The solution for making an unsinkable ship turned out to be a problem compounding everyone's chances at survival.

Some of those who have examined this disaster have even speculated that if there had not been any bulkheads, the ship would have actually stayed afloat *longer*, thereby potentially allowing other ships to reach the sinking vessel. They might even have been in time to save its passengers and crew.

We can learn a lesson from this, dads. Just because it seems like a good idea, it doesn't mean that it won't lead to disaster. Good ideas can backfire. New and liberal ideas on fathering, along with hard-nosed traditionalism, can both seem like good ideas. Fathers fall prey to the traditions and half-truths they received from their fathers and that have been passed down from generation to generation—traditions and ideas that seem right, but in truth are tragically flawed. And as with the *Titanic*, if we don't check these ideas, they can sink our home.

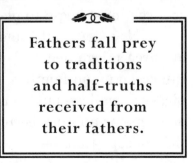

Fathers fall prey
to traditions
and half-truths
received from
their fathers.

Are you one of those men? Are you one of those whose ideas could sink your home? Would you like to know how you can tell? If you would like to know whether or not your ideas on fathering might actually spell your family's disaster, here's how you can check to make sure you don't have some major design flaws.

Take inventory of your family right now. How does it stack up? Are you satisfied with everything you see, or are there some chinks in the armor? Is your family whole, or are there some holes in your family?

Close this book for a minute and really think—take the time for real, brutally honest introspection. You need to make another decision, dad: will you continue to travel in the same path you've been on, or will you set your heart and mind to change your family for good no matter the cost?

You see, we are where we are today because of what we planted yesterday; and we will harvest tomorrow—and beyond—what we plant today. So where are you? Where's your family? If you don't like what you see, you must begin to plant different seeds.

Now, let's put some legs to this truth. Let's look at three misguided and potentially deadly flaws that can creep up on families. One of the bigger—if not the biggest—wall we put up is one that many men have at one time or another become ensnared by. This flaw is the concept that being a *workaholic* is "good for the family." It's the notion that being at work all the time is right and necessary. It's thinking, "Well, you have to make some sacrifices to build up that nest egg." And family time came out on the short end of the stick. How about this one—"There certainly is a price to pay to get to the top!" Yes, there certainly is a price to pay; and rest assured your family doesn't have enough to cover the cost!

The underlying idea is that if you work yourself to death now, you'll be able to spend time with your family later—when you can afford it. It's another one of those naïve thoughts, and if you really believe this one, it's probably safe to say that the water might be coming over the top of your walls already and beginning to sink your family.

A number of years ago, a friend of mine lamented to me that he had basically missed half of his young son's life simply because of his work and travel schedule. *Half!* He realized that these were years that he would never, ever be able to get back. The precious time of playing or reading or talking or just dreaming with his child was just flat out *gone.*

And it's not just about the time he missed; it's about what he could have been putting into his son during that time—it was time that he could have poured into his son physically, mentally, emotionally, and spiritually. He could have created, developed, constructed, led, influenced, and mentored his son as he grew up, but instead, he ultimately left that to someone else. *That* was the job he was supposed to be doing, but some bad wiring in his thinking had him believing he was supposed to be in the office or on the road when he was supposed to be being a father.

Thankfully, his wife—like so many others—did an excellent job picking up the slack, but what about those stories that don't have a faithful spouse to fill in the blanks that dad left? What about those kids that are left in front of the television or in the streets? What about those kids? What about *your* kids?

This flaw—missing time with your child because of overemphasis on pleasing the boss instead of playing with the boy—is a design flaw that sinks families every day, one child at a time. Come on dads, what kind of job is so important that it's worth damaging your family? *None*!

Regardless of what our job description or title might be, neither can compare to the one you've been given—dad. Yeah, you might get that promotion, but if it comes at the price of a damaged family, let it be someone else's prize so your family doesn't.

Now, I'm not anti-job or against hard work. All should work to the best of their ability and be responsible. I am just saying that if it ever becomes a choice as to which one wins—job or family—we have to buck the trend of picking our families second!

In Steve Martin's remake of the classic family movie *Cheaper by the Dozen,* he plays a college football coach who gets the job of his dreams; yet like so many other jobs, it takes a heavy toll on his family. At the end of the movie, he makes his choice to regain his family. The athletic director asks him if he's really going to give up his dream, and Steve Martin looks his boss squarely in the eye and proclaims that if he messes up raising his children, then nothing else really matters!

Would that we as men were a lot more concerned about our families and less about our dreams! Once again, there is nothing wrong with possessing a passionate vision or men pursuing the right dreams, but listen closely, dads. Let's make sure that the biggest dreams in our homes are not of our *families* dreaming that we weren't so busy!

Another thing about your job: There are times when any career path might go through times of heavy workloads, difficult schedules, and frequent travel. Sometimes that's just part of life, but never let that become an excuse for not spending time with your family. And when work seems hectic and crazy, let's not forget to sacrifice some of our own leisure time to make up for the time we missed with our family.

Here's another concept that's flawed, and this one is just as bad as the first. It's the idea that children are resilient. You've heard it said before: children are resilient! Yes they can bounce back from some trauma, but the real truth is that children aren't resilient, they're *impressionable.*

I am truly appalled with the notion that children can take verbal, emotional, or even physical shots or have destruction planted in their lives because their parents think their children are resilient. The hurts children are encouraged to shake off have a lasting impact on their future! They hurt when it happens, and these injuries leave scars and damage behind. Think about this, dads: we mold, craft, and make our children's destinies every day.

People that hide behind this reasoning have truly become deceived. Let's get brutally honest—if you really believe kids are resilient and can stomach pain and heartache without suffering long-term effects, you're not only cruising for a family disaster, start bailing the water because your home is already sinking. Kids get hurt; they form lasting scars and just don't bounce back without some mark on their soul—be it little or large. Resilient? Not likely. Impressionable? Absolutely.

Just Say No

The third flaw is really brutal because it might not come back to do any damage until years later. The need for caution and serious forethought is so important here! Sometimes being the nice guy and always saying "yes" to your children is a mistake. It's a faulty piece of engineering to think that if you always give them what they want they'll be happy.

I once listened to a man as he told of his family's new challenge. His brokenness was extremely evident as he shared how his tears had flowed as he thought about the fate of his oldest daughter. In the eyes of the world, this man is a winner, but he lamented not only about his family's current troubles but more importantly about what had taken place in the past that got them to where they were.

He had just found out that his unwed daughter was pregnant. Together with her ongoing drug addiction, it was a recipe for a brokenhearted father and family.

As he solemnly described to me his family's heartache, he began to give me words of warning that I can never forget. He had recently retired in his early forties as a multimillionaire, but he was realizing that no amount of money in the world could take away his hurt or pain. His company had grown from ten to over ten thousand employees and had offices around the world. And even though he was brilliant at building a financial empire, he had come to realize that his fathering skills had come up severely lacking.

He said, "Jim Moore, you had better listen. Ten years ago, I was going top speed—yet I was asleep at the wheel."

He then related something profound—the most important word in parenting is the word "no." He said that during his kids' lives, he wanted to be the fun dad. He said he just wanted their family to have fun.

He ended by quietly and humbly saying, "We're not having fun now." He had built a business from zero to a zillion, and he now faced the fact that there's more to life than a balance sheet and that building a family was more important than building a fortune.

The night of the wreck, *Titanic* was traveling at top speed in an iceberg field; when I think about that, I just ask myself, "Why?" What was

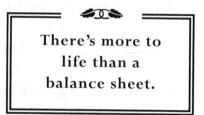

There's more to life than a balance sheet.

so important that it made those in charge do what they did and make the type of decisions that they made? Could it have possibly been that a lot of pressure was put on those in charge to persuade them to make those choices, or was it just standard procedure to knowingly run that way through iceberg fields?

In James Cameron's movie, you're left with the thought that Captain Smith was pressured. The real truth lies buried in the hearts of men and at the bottom of the ocean. Who really knows? I have read accounts and words supporting both sides but here's what I want to ask you: what if they did give in to pressure?

You can read the Senate inquiry notes and find that at least three messages got to Captain Smith before the wreck, and you can find out that before he went to bed, he said he wanted to be contacted should they run into any ice. So what does that tell us?

Let's note that there isn't a single dad on the face of the earth who hasn't at one time or another caved in to the pressure of the world. No one is going to debate this, but here's what we've got to do, dads.

We've got to learn when to pick our battles and when to take our stand with our kids and clearly learn to say the word "no." It might not win us the Parent of the Day award from our kids, but it just might save ourselves and our families from some worldly entanglements that seek to destroy.

Sometimes the word "no" can be the most positive thing you can say! Let's learn that one now, dads, before it's too late.

Flawed ideas are dangerous. Unless we're willing to take the time to evaluate ourselves and unless we're willing to get uncompromisingly honest with ourselves in order to make any necessary changes, we might not notice the fatal nature of our errors until it's often too late.

Parents need to be experts in crisis prevention, not crisis reaction. You don't want to discover your faulty ideas when the water starts pouring over the walls.

There is a huge difference, however, between just checking for flaws and changing the faulty ideas that can sink your family. Anyone who even remotely cares about his family can easily stop and go through some mental exercise to see how his family is doing, but it takes a real man—a real father committed to becoming the dad he was destined to be—to change anything it takes to preserve his family.

Checking up on ourselves takes really no accountability or effort, but changing—now that takes a man's man to accomplish such a feat. The question is, are we all willing to be that man? Flawed engineering or family excellence: the choice is ours!

ACTION POINTS

1. Take a moment to think of three things that you wish your father had done better in raising you. Honestly consider how your children would rate you on these same issues. If you think they'd rate you poorly, take a moment to think of a way to help yourself get better in each category.

2. Ask your family where they think your priorities are—your job or them? Rest assured—-they will probably tell you!

3. Are you committed to having a spiritual relationship with your Heavenly Father in order to make you a better earthly father? Dedicate some of your quiet times with God to reflecting on the model of a Father He presents to us dads.

CHAPTER TEN

TURN BACK BEFORE
THE SCREAMS DIE OUT

His name was Harold Godfrey Lowe. He left home in his teens and after much training found himself years later an experienced sailor. Over time, he climbed the ranks, and as fate would have it, he received the honor to become the *Titanic's* fifth officer for its maiden voyage.

That particular tragic Sunday night, he had gone to bed early and was later awakened not by the crash but by the sound of passengers outside his room. After getting dressed, he assisted with loading passengers into various lifeboats and was ultimately given charge of a lifeboat himself. Once lowered into the water, he directed his vessel to about 150 yards away from the sinking *Titanic*, rounded up several other boats, and began to redistribute passengers into other lifeboats.

Then Lowe did something very difficult. Now pay attention. He positioned his lifeboat just far enough away from the wreck that he could still hear the screams of the hundreds of passengers who were in the water, hopelessly clinging to anything that could float. And he waited for those screams to die down—and soon they did.

Think about it: men and women, boys and girls, grandmas and grandpas. It didn't matter if they were young or old, rich or poor. That night the destruction from the wreck was no respecter of persons nor played any favorites to its victims and as a result of this senseless mess, destinies were shortened and descendants were scarred. When Lowe felt it was safe to go back and look for survivors, he returned and found four.

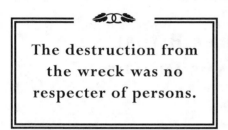

The destruction from the wreck was no respecter of persons.

Later at the Senate hearing that dealt with the sinking of the *Titanic*, he was grilled by Senator Smith about his decision to fall back and just wait. According to Lowe, it was necessary because in his opinion, had he rowed his boat back among the hundreds of freezing passengers, they all would have rushed the lifeboats, sinking all of them, and causing everyone to die. What a horrible situation! So he sat, waited, and listened.

Now stop for a moment. Try to put yourself in his shoes. It's pitch black, you're in the middle of a freezing North Atlantic with thousands of miles of water all around you and nothing but a wooden lifeboat between you and certain death. You've just witnessed the greatest ship in the world sink. You have fifty people or so in your boat, and more surrounding you—and you hear the screams. Bloodcurdling, desperate cries of people who are taking some of their life's last breaths and fighting for every one. And you realize that if you dare go back and begin to pick up survivors, you could never even begin to rescue them all. And not only that, you also know that once you go back, those rightfully desperate, panic-stricken people calling for help, will probably swamp your boat.

What would you do? There's a term that describes this kind of dilemma: it's called "situational ethics." Here's the peril that he faced—attempt to rescue some and possibly lose all, or decide to rescue who you know you can save and let the others perish? If he goes back they might *all* die—those in the water and those in his boat. If he doesn't go back, all those in the water die. What would *you* do? There is simply no way we can truly imagine the anguish that must have been going through Lowe's mind. His move—or lack thereof—will probably be debated for many years to come.

A million people could read about his decision and come up with their own solutions, but Lowe surveyed the situation and made what he felt was the best choice. That decision was to stay away and wait for the screams to die down, knowing that would be his sign that it was safe to go back in and look for a few souls that could still be saved. And he did just that.

Now fathers, here's the point: every day, too many dads see their own dreams crash on an unexpected iceberg and sink. If you're one of those dads, perhaps you've moved off to what you think of as a safe distance from your family; and I'm not going to debate the situational ethics of your choice. The question is what you're going to do about the screams you're hearing.

The voices are familiar; they're of your family, and they're within range. Maybe you can see them. Maybe you're a hundred and fifty yards away, a hundred and fifty miles away, or even fifteen hundred miles away; but one thing is for sure—you know they're there and that they're in trouble. You can sense it in your soul, and you can hear them in your heart.

They are hanging on to anything or anyone that they hope will keep them afloat, and they are calling out for you, dad, to come back and rescue them! They *saw you leave*. They watched and panicked as you paddled away to a safe distance for yourself, and they're in the icy waters,

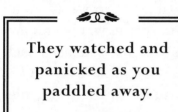

They watched and panicked as you paddled away.

wondering why you did it and if you are ever coming back.

Are you? They are calling out for you to rescue them from a world of vices, snares, and pitfalls that can certainly swallow them as surely as if they were in the ice cold North Atlantic—unless you intervene.

And the same question that called out to Harold Godfrey Lowe in 1912 now calls out to you today: *what will you do?*

Obviously your family isn't *literally* in the frigid North Atlantic, and this isn't 1912 anymore. No one should judge Harold Lowe for his decision. As a matter of fact, he was the only one who went back to look for survivors. The truth is that Lowe should have never been placed in that position—had those in charge done their duty and heeded the warnings they had received all day, no one would have been in the water. If some people had not thought even God couldn't sink their ship, they would have had more lifeboats. To judge Harold Lowe would be a mistake, but the failure to judge your own heart would be an even greater one.

The biggest question right now might not be how you got to where you are today—although you must deal with that one very quickly—but instead, what are you going to do to reconcile you and your home? Lowe had rowed out, but something in him made him stop and

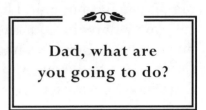

Dad, what are you going to do?

go back to deal with what he found. This might be true with you, too, dad. You're going to have to decide, and every moment you hesitate brings those left in the water closer to destruction.

By the time the *Carpathia* arrived on the morning of April 15, those in the water were all dead; and tragically, in many instances, by the time another rescuer comes to intervene on behalf of your family, they might simply arrive too late. Dad, what are you going to do?

How many Christmases that you missed have you lamented in your heart that you weren't there to open presents with them? How many birthday parties must pass by without you before you change your mind and go back?

Tragically, there are many fathers who *can't* go back for one reason or another. Many times, because of the judicial system in our country, fathers are not afforded the right to raise or even *see* their children. These dads have been removed from the situation by forces they often could not fight against even if they wanted to. This illustration is in **no way** geared towards you. But for those of you who are free to act, this illustration of survivors in the water is for you.

Maybe you went away in fear; maybe you chose to pursue your selfish ambitions or turned your back on your family out of a misplaced sense of priorities. Maybe you flat-out quit. I hope that as you search yourself, you will realize, just as Harold Lowe did, that you must go back. However, understand that if you wait for the screams to die out, you might just be too late! You don't have to wait for the screams to stop—nor should you.

Dad—that is still your name—can you hear them? Maybe you've tried to drown them out with the sounds of preoccupation, or success, or the sounds of hammers pounding away as you try to build your new kingdom. But you can't and I don't think you'll ever be able to. Personally, I don't think any distance or any attempt to drown out the sounds can silence that conviction within you that they desperately need you!

We are often capable of forging ahead and creating a place of safety for ourselves. We're officers on our own ship, and we're in command of our own personal lifeboats. You might survive the crash, dad, but would you leave your family in the icy waters while you're safe in a boat? Would you even leave them on the *Titanic*? Of course you wouldn't! It's time to be honest and ask yourself why you left them at all.

Maybe you've already pushed off and are at your safe distance, but I hope that something in you will make you go back, even if you left them to save yourself. Like Harold Godfrey Lowe listening from a safe distance in a boat, you too can still hear them. Maybe you're afraid. Maybe you think that they might not ever be able to forgive you because you paddled away. You panicked; you weren't thinking clearly, and now you're thinking that you made the wrong choice and you're not sure how to find your way back.

Here's how you do it: *you start by paddling back toward the screams.*

You might be thinking, "It's not that easy," or, "You don't know my situation." You're right on both counts, but how are you ever going to salvage them if you stay away? Harold Lowe didn't fully know what he was going to find when he went back, but there were two things I bet he knew. First, I bet he was convinced there were some who saw him leave; and second, he knew that they all needed him to come back. They saw you leave, dad, and whether you realize it or not, they need you to come back.

One last thought: I bet that long after the night of April 14, Lowe could still hear the screams. If it were me, I'm not sure I'd ever be able to get the screams out of my mind, especially in the dark hours when you're alone with them. Dad, if you stay away, I really believe you will hear those screams for the rest of your life one way or another. You will hear their screams for the rest of your life if there is any humanity in you at all.

It's time to turn back your vessel. It's now time to go back to where you got off course and entered into what you thought would be safer water. It's time to go back to your family. It's time to head back to the screams—before they die out. *It's time.*

Can you hear them? Are you listening? What are you going to do?

In James Cameron's movie, *Titanic*, Lowe's character is seen going back to look for survivors, and in the midst of all the human carnage in the ocean he comes across a mother and her child who were floating in the water. They froze to death. After surveying the carnage in the water, Lowe says out loud to himself, "We waited too long." Dad, please don't let those words ever become yours.

ACTION POINTS

1. Have you left your family alone—physically or emotionally—and in trouble? List three problems that your family members are possibly going through right now, big or small, and come up with one idea about how you can help in even a small way in each of them.

2. When was the last time you sacrificed some desire of yours that was so big that your children knew about it and it strengthened their relationship with you? If it's been a while, pick something important to you, cancel it, and spend time with your family instead—and make that plan today!

3. Have you physically or emotionally left your wife in the wake of your pursuit of your dreams? Don't just tell her you're sorry; show it with your actions. Begin to show her again that she is truly important to you.

CHAPTER ELEVEN

WHEN DAD'S NOT THERE

When I was growing up in a small town in west Texas, it was easy to find my dad. All you had to do was to look for our family and you would find Louie Moore there. He was (and still is) the consummate family man—an excellent husband and devoted father. My sister and I are extremely fortunate in that, unlike many kids across America today, we had a family story that is positive.

Our father is loving, caring, and was very good at discipline. As a matter of fact, one of my favorite impressions to do is of him ripping off his belt from his pants as he prepared to dismantle folly from our heart through the padding of our backsides. You've never seen smoke coming from a pair of Sansabelts until you've seen Louie Moore yanking off his belt at just under Mach two. When I heard those belt loops popping, I knew what my immediate fate was, and even though it was painful, he did not fail to impart the fact that it was ultimately for my good. Such was the discipline of my father. Yet when he wasn't being forced to correct his kids, he proved his love and commitment to us over and over again by constantly being there for us when we needed him.

My father never carried a fancy title at his job. He never held an executive position and certainly wasn't born on third base; as a matter of fact, he was born on a farm in west Texas and grew up dirt poor. We never heard him complaining about the circumstances he was born into. He never played the blame game, and he never cursed his fate or his father. What we heard were the cheers of our dad spurring us on to be our best. He was and still is my hero. In short, he's great. Perfect—no. Great—absolutely! Superman—probably not, although now that I think about it, I never have seen the two of them in the same room at the same time!

Ken Canfield wrote an excellent piece for the Web site of the National Center for Fathering about the value of investing time into our children. He gives the example of what would happen if we were given $86,400.00 at the beginning of each day. The only rule was that you had to wisely spend each dollar each day, because when the clock struck midnight whatever money you had not spent evaporated. None of it carried over.

If that scenario were true today, we as fathers would have a blast trying to spend that much dough before it was lost, and I dare say we wouldn't miss many opportunities to fulfill the day's task. But the reality of it is that each day we have been given a greater investment to be a steward of—the investment of time. Eighty-six thousand four hundred seconds per day to be exact. We have 86,400 seconds a day to make a positive difference in this world, and 86,400 seconds to attempt to make the lives of our family members successful and to show them our love. And with apologies to my third grade

You spell it T-I-M-E!

teacher, Mrs. Lippard, you don't spell love L-O-V-E. You spell it T-I-M-E!

My father proved that concept to be true, because he was always there at every event. He was always supporting and cheering us on, and he did a little coaching as well. He was always at my games. When I first started playing Pee Wee League baseball, he even went one step further than just attending—he was my coach.

For those who might not know this, a pee wee coach's job might just be the roughest in the world. You're dealing with kids who have probably never played much baseball, so it is not a glamorous job, and all the while you have to deal with the parents that think their son should be starting at shortstop.

Yet every year that I played—or should I say "attempted to play" baseball—I could count on my father being my coach and my mentor. As I grew older and began to play junior high football, he was there too. I would be standing on the sideline, (I did do a lot of that in my sporting career), and I would look to find him. And he would be there in the crowd, cheering on his son. As I grew older and continued to play more and more sports, his consistent and faithful attendance never wavered.

And one of the most interesting things about him being at all my games is that he wasn't some executive that could dictate his schedule and come and go as he pleased. Yet he always made sure that if a game was during the day, he found a way to be there.

He *made* the time.

This all leads me to the only game I can ever remember him missing. It was around Christmas of my junior year in high school, and we were playing one of the best teams in the state. They were in our conference, so it was a pivotal game for our season. I had been fortunate enough to make the varsity team, but because I was still an underclassman, I played the first half of the junior varsity game to gather game experience and then found my usual seat on the bench and watched the upperclassmen play in the varsity game. As I said, it was around Christmas, and I believe my parents had some type of work conflict that kept the two of them from traveling to the out of town event.

I will never forget that night—nor will my parents. It was in the first half of the junior varsity game, and I was running up the court when all of a sudden this guy on the opposing team, running behind me, tripped me. I fell face first onto the floor—and then to add injury to insult, he kicked me in the back of the head, which caused my face to smash straight into the hardwood floor, knocking me silly.

As I laid there right in front of the opposing team's cheerleading section, I realized that I was hurt and was in some serious facial pain. I also found out by the comments from the girls in the pom-pom section that I was not their favorite person in the world. As a matter of fact, it seemed that there was this one particular shrieking voice in that section that was enjoying seeing me in obvious pain!

When I came to my senses and got to my feet, I realized that something wasn't right. It seemed as if my nose was able to smell my left ear, and then I realized that my nose had been broken! Sure enough, the next day the doctor made a startling diagnosis and gave me the official word—yes, it was broken. I guess it was the fact that my nose was in the shape of an "S" that probably gave it away.

So as you might imagine, I wasn't in a particularly good mood the rest of the evening, especially since some of my teammates thought it was absolutely hilarious to see a nose that close to an ear on the same face. As the night progressed, so did my pain, which made my level of having a good attitude about life sink even lower.

I will never forget, as we were preparing to go out and play the varsity game, our head coach made one thing perfectly clear: he wanted those on the bench, (I definitely qualified for that one), to "Keep your mouth shut and do not pick up a technical foul." I found that statement extremely out of character for our head coach. I played for this guy for three years, heard dozens of pre-, half-, and post-game speeches, and this was the only time that he had ever made that type of comment. And it was such a waste of time for him to make such an outlandish statement, because this was, after all, a high school basketball game in the '70s, and if there was one thing you don't get in a high school game it's a technical foul—and especially from the bench! Right!

Well...I was in a lot of pain, and we were in the first half of a heated battle. I mean, this was *the* team in the state to beat, and they had one of the greatest players in the state. He went on to become an all-conference player in college and, in my opinion, was probably the best shooter our college team had ever seen. (He also went on to be one of my best friends in college.) Anyway, it was a heated battle, and it was a close game. And then it happened. One of the officials made what, in my opinion, could have gone down as one of the worst calls in the history of high school basketball.

Did I mention that I was in a lot of pain? And I just felt that someone needed to take it upon himself to, in a nice and polite way, describe to Mr. Official that he had just missed a critical call that hurt our momentum. I mean, come on—he was ten feet from it, and I was easily 110 feet from it with a crooked nose and a bad attitude! If I could see it, then surely he could too! To this day, I will never fully understand how he picked out my voice out of a jam-packed gymnasium with a band, hundreds of fans, both teams, cheerleaders, and a pom-pom squad (with one particularly loud obnoxious person in it) from the rest...but he did.

Did I mention the fact that I was in lots of pain? There are many things I would like to forget about that night, but there are two that I will probably never be able to. First, I will remember for a long time how badly I wanted to find a hole to crawl into as I saw my head coach begin his journey down the bench to find out which of his players with a nose shaped like an "S" couldn't keep his mouth shut and had actually picked up a technical foul—"from the bench."

And the second thing I would like to forget was what our play-by-play radio announcer said when I received the technical: "And a technical foul has just been called on the Springdale bench!" I found out about this because, as fate would have it, my mom and dad had found their way to a radio just in time to hear those words.

No one knew who the technical foul was on other than the official who pointed it out to my head coach, my coach, myself, and the other players who were probably pointing straight at me. They never called my name over the radio. No one should have been able to figure it out—no one except Louie and Teenie Moore. But that night, the radar that most parents have was working perfectly—you know, that radar that tells them you messed up before you have a chance to explain why you messed up? My mother and father knew it was me, and as they heard the radio announcer make his comment, they said out loud to each other, "When he gets home tonight we're going to kill him!" They just knew it was me!

Now, you might ask, "Where in the world are you going with this one?" Good question. The example I am trying to make is this: the only night my dad wasn't there to watch me was the same night I got hurt and also got into trouble. Now, I'm not saying that if Louie Moore would have been at the game it would have turned out any differently for my nose, but I believe it would have turned out much differently for my big mouth. Because I do know that I would have done a much better job of keeping it shut if I knew that my dad was sitting behind me in the stands. I probably would not have picked up the "T."

I'd like to take this opportunity to say a word here about personal accountability and responsibility. The bottom line is that it's ultimately the child's choice on what he or she does, and your child has to live with that decision. But let's get down to the bare essentials. For children to have any chance at all to avoid destruction, it is necessary that you raise and teach them correctly. Remember, fathers, what we sow into our children's hearts and minds will come to the surface in their lives.

My story is merely anecdotal, but I simply find it an interesting coincidence that the night dad was not around, bad things happened. And here's the lesson; hear it well, dads: when we are not around, our kids can get hurt or into trouble—or both—and it's no laughing matter. Keep a close watch, dad, because their destiny might just be hanging in the balance—when you're not around, bad things can happen to your family.

Keep a close watch, dad.

Oh, and P.S.—I love you, Dad!

ACTION POINTS

1. When was the last time you specifically marked out a day on your calendar for an event of your child? If you can't remember, do it now!

2. Are your children growing up with the sense of security that you'll support them and be the biggest cheerleader in their lives? Make a point of being at their next event and to be the loudest positive voice cheering them on! Write it in your day timer if you have to!

3. Are you an encourager or a critic in their lives? If the latter, write down three things per child that you can encourage them on in a day—and do it every day!

CHAPTER TWELVE

TWO DADS—TWO DESTINIES

The early morning hours of April 15, 1912 saw many lives lost in the freezing North Atlantic, but it also saw hundreds of people rescued because of the incredible bravery of some dedicated people. Here is the story of one such man.

At the beginning of the book, I introduced you to a man named Frederick Fleet, the one who actually first spotted the iceberg. When I began to research the story of this man's life, I was amazed and at the same time saddened by what I found. His life story is of a man who, from birth throughout his years and even until his death, was abandoned and neglected, and it paints a picture of what the end result of a lifetime of hurt can be.

He was deserted by both parents so from his earliest days, seeds of inattention and abandonment were planted into his life. Do yourself a favor and stop and think about what I just said. Did you just gloss over it and not even think about the impact on the child? With today's nonchalant and calloused attitude toward the family, it's easy to just pass over the concept of an un-fathered child, but in reality it is absolutely horrible!

From his earliest days until his death, seeds of hurt, neglect, shame, inattention, and abandonment were planted into his life. Those early years of development, where his heart was shaped and his soul was molded, were done so without him ever having the blessings from his mother or father. Like too many innocent kids today, there was possibly a huge deficit in his heart that could not be satisfied. And similar to what happens too often today, growing up without one or both parents can potentially leave such a void in a child's life that—unless it's dealt with successfully—can produce a lot of internal strife, which can lead to an external destruction.

Frederick never knew what it was like to have his father around—playing with him, teaching him, modeling manhood to him, and just hanging out with him. He never heard his dad say, "I love you" or, "Great job son, I'm really proud of you!" Maybe you didn't, either, and you're now waking up to the alarming fact that you're passing down those same deadly tendencies to your own children; you're shocked that it has crept up on you. Remember, it's called drifting—drifting from what you know is the right thing to do. It's time for you to radically get connected again as best you can and as your circumstances will allow.

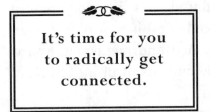

It's time for you to radically get connected.

Back to Frederick; he also never knew what it was like to be held by his mom when he needed it most. There was no bonding in his early years, no kiss from her when he was tucked in at night. He never felt her tender, loving care and he never heard the words in a way that only moms can say it—"I love you." He never had that chance.

What kind of wound is punctured into a child's heart when he or she lives that kind of life? I believe it's the kind that sometimes never heals, the kind that can leave noticeable scars. He spent those formative years living in different homes. Possibly more seeds of abandonment, inattention, and shame planted into his life. When he got older he started his nautical training. Growing up at sea just seemed to be his destiny, and when he was twenty-four, he got the opportunity to join the White Star line as a lookout on the *Titanic*.

The good news about Frederick was that he survived the wreck; the bad news was that he survived the wreck. As a crewman, if you survived the *Titanic* disaster in 1912, some people actually thought you were an embarrassment to the White Star line. In some peoples' eyes, it would have been better for him to go down with the ship. About twenty minutes after the collision, he came down from his post and was given responsibility of assisting with Lifeboat #6. He took women and children to safety, including "the Unsinkable Molly Brown." The next morning, they were rescued by the *Carpathia*.

Later on, he testified before Congress about the wreck and was asked if the outcome of the journey would have been different had he had a pair of binoculars with him in the crow's nest. In Frederick's mind, it seems as though it was clear that if he would have had the proper equipment, the entire disaster *could* have been avoided. None of this senseless tragedy had to happen, but it *did* happen. The tragedy, along with the "what ifs" and second-guessing probably planted and cultivated more seeds of shame into his life.

So for the next half century, he probably carried some of that load on his shoulders. We find him selling newspapers late in his life, and in 1964 his wife passed away. A few days later, Frederick did what he may have felt was the only thing left to do with his life—he took it.

His body was laid to rest in an unmarked grave, and after his death his Seaman's Discharge Book was found—the world could know what the famous Frederick Fleet wrote about that Sunday night in 1912. He penned two lines—simple yet incredibly profound: Discharged at sea—destination intended for New York.

Did you catch that, dads? Discharged at sea—destination intended for New York. In other words, there was a grand plan laid out for over 2200 people on board. They were supposed to be part of history, yet because of self-inflicted mistakes along the way, many plans and lives were lost. Does that sound familiar, dad? Does it sound like the story of your family?

Every life and every family begins its journey with a destiny. Dreams of success and happiness. Dreams that were charted out long before the journey began, yet your fathering eyes have not been functioning properly, and perhaps some needless collisions have occurred? Dads, before those wrecks that aren't repairable occur, we need to consider the destiny that lies before us and vow to do whatever we need to do to see our entire household remain on course and collision free.

I realize that many who read this will have already seen some (and sometimes what appear to be all) of your dreams dashed. Maybe you've begun to take on water, and you're looking for an answer to repair the damage.

Here is one solution: years ago, there was a man named Jonah who, because of his own neglect, literally found himself in the belly of a huge fish. While he was in that awful mess, he had some time to think and consider his life. (I mean, what else can you do in the belly of a fish? There's obviously no television or golf course.) As he was there, he began to consider his ways.

The instructions he'd received were simple—he was to go in a certain direction to a certain town, but like many people, he didn't heed the call and traveled in another direction. Along the way, his cruise ship hit a great storm, and like many of *Titanic's* passengers, he found himself in the water without a raft. Upon considering his poor choices, he proclaimed, "Those who cling to worthless idols forfeit the grace that could be theirs."

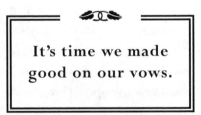

It's time we made good on our vows.

Then, upon coming to the conclusion that obedience to the original call was the right thing to do, he simply said, "What I have vowed I will make good." Did you catch that, dad? What I have vowed I will make good.

It's time we made good on our vows.

Dads, what worthless idols have we clung to and have made us let go of important things? What vows have you made that you have forgotten about that have caused you to sink and become fish food? Whatever they are, now is the time for us to reconsider our ways and once again do what we have committed to do. When you got married, you committed yourself to being a leader in your relationship, and when that marriage produced children, you were committing yourself to raising them. Make good on your vows, dad.

Think about the very first time you ever held your baby boy or girl. Think about the indescribable thoughts of love, compassion, and the utter sense of humility you felt. This was a new life that you helped create! Well, guess what? Creating a life and forming a destiny doesn't stop at birth; it actually has just begun. It's time to revisit those plans again and make good the vows you made to your family at one time.

Dads, even though you might be thinking that it's past the point of no return and that anything you might do would be useless, let me encourage you to reconsider your ways and do what you can to repair the damage in a positive way! It begins with renewing your mind, creating a new plan of action, and possibly a large dose of humility. And it doesn't matter if your child is two or fifty-two, you alone have the ability to fulfill your vows and hopefully see your family through to its intended destiny.

A Father to the Rescue

Eighty years after *Titanic*, a man named Derek Redmond, a world-class athlete going for the gold in the Olympic Games in Barcelona, Spain, generated a ton of human interest stories. Four years earlier, he was actually hoping to win the gold in the 1988 Olympics but just before he was to go to the blocks and race, he had to withdraw because of an injury to his Achilles.

For those of you who know something about athletics, you probably know that if you injure your Achilles seriously enough, many times your athletic career is finished. But four years and several surgeries later, he found himself not only just in rehabilitation training, he had worked and trained himself back into shape—and into the '92 Olympic games.

This time Derek got stretched out, and a few moments later the starter fired the gun and the race began. All appeared to be going well until shortly into the race when Derek suddenly suffered a hamstring injury and hit the track. He was obviously in agony, but the race continued. A few moments later, the winner crossed the finish line, but most—if not all—the eyes in the stadium and many of those watching by television saw something they could not believe and would not soon forget.

They watched as Derek Redmond got himself up to his feet and began to hobble to the finish line. I read one article that interviewed Derek; he said the reason he began to attempt to reach the finish line was because he was so focused on the race, he truly thought he could catch the competitors—though they had already finished the race.

As he was struggling along, something so incredible happened, you would just have to see it to truly catch the magnitude of it. A man came down from the stands and tried to get to Derek. He had come from another part of the stadium. He hurried down all those steps and then scaled over a wall to get down onto the stadium floor to reach Derek. A security guard tried to apprehend the man, since you obviously don't want spectators to run onto the stadium floor to get to an athlete. But this man threw the security guard to the side and actually made it to Derek. He put his arms around the runner, as if to help him. Derek, still focused on finishing and not knowing who it was, pushed his arms away until he heard the man say, "Derek, it's me."

Derek looked up to see Jim Redmond, his dad. Jim looked into his son's eyes, which were grimacing with pain, and said, "You don't have to do this." Derek looked at his father and said, "Yes, I do."

Jim Redmond looked at his son and said, "Well then, we're going to finish this together." He put his arms around his son, he kept him in the right lane, and they finished the race together.

Now, dads, you listen to this: that particular day, Derek Redmond didn't win the gold medal, but he learned that he possessed something far more valuable. He left with the knowledge that his daddy was willing to fight his way to get to him when he saw his son in pain. He let nothing stop him from reaching his son. He put his arms around him, spoke words of life into him, kept him in the right lane, and finished the race with him.

Dads, tonight children are crying out for a father who will see them in their pain and come to them, a father who will leave his seat in the stands and get out of his comfort zone. They need someone who will race to them, put his arms around them, and do everything he can to keep them on track so they can finish the race together.

Dads, we seem to have yet to learn there's a difference between those who just start something and those who actually *finish*. There is a lot of difference between a man who does his part in creating a child and a man who follows his children through to mold their young hearts into those of modern-day champions.

Come on dads, there's a whole lot of fathers who have given in to the useless mold of this world that says that it's not that big a deal for you not to be involved in your children's lives. You've caved to the pressure, and you've painted a clear picture to your kids that they're not that important to you. Maybe you didn't paddle away, but you're certainly not giving them the type of fathering they desperately desire and deserve.

We started this chapter by talking about two different men with two different experiences. Frederick Fleet's father abandoned him; Derek Redmond's father helped him to finish. One man was tossed aside from the beginning; the other man had help in his life but especially when it counted most. Frederick's father showed him he wasn't worth the effort, and Derek's dad showed he was worth struggle and sacrifice. One paddled away, not even listening for the screams; the other raced to his son's side because he saw the pain.

Which one are you? Which one do you want to be? I don't know anything about Derek or his father other than what I read, but on the day of the race, you had to be impressed by what you witnessed.

Fathering is a unique and somewhat mysterious task set before us, but make no mistake about it, it is set before us, and we will be called into account for how well we do it. The choice is ours. Our choices will affect our family's destiny—possibly for generations to come!

ACTION POINTS

1. When was the last time you left work or cancelled any of your recreation to tend to your child when they were home from school sick? Make a note to do that next time instead of expecting your wife to do it.

2. Do you pray for your children daily? Even if you have to write out a schedule, start praying for your children—and start today, right now!

3. Are you a "closet father," or do your buddies know that you're a committed dad? Make a point of choosing your family over them for a while, and see if your family and your friends notice the change.

CHAPTER THIRTEEN

LIFESAVING LESSONS

The ship's name was *Carpathia*. She left port from New York almost the same day that the *Titanic* took off from South Hampton headed to New York. This thirteen hundred ton ship had the capacity to carry around twenty-five hundred passengers, but on this particular voyage, it was not at capacity. As fate would have it, those hundreds of spaces would soon be filled with unsuspecting passengers from another ship. Little did the crew of *Carpathia* know that this seemingly routine journey to the Mediterranean would soon become a lifesaving venture for so many.

The captain of the *Carpathia* was Arthur Henry Rostron. Everything I have read about this man leads me to believe that he was a man of standing. His character and compassion shown through as he later testified at the Congressional Hearings about the wreck, and his replaying of those last hours of the rescue mission brought tears to many who heard it. He was a man of concern and he was a man of faith.

Captain Rostron did a lot of heroic things and saved the lives of so many. He was awakened after midnight by Harold Cottam, his wireless operator, after Cottam received the distress call from *Titanic*. After hearing about the disaster, he instructed Cottam to relay this message: "Tell them we're coming as fast as we can." He then began his charting and determined the course and the approximate time they would reach the wreck. He later said that he charted the course while he was dressing.

The mission that lay ahead was instantly apparent to him, and he began to instruct his crew to focus on the critical issue at hand. He even instructed that the heat and the hot water be cut off so more steam could be thrust into the boilers in the hopes that their speed would pick up and they would be able to reach the doomed ship in time. *Carpathia* was running so hard and fast her decks were throbbing!

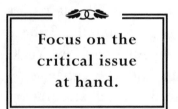

Focus on the critical issue at hand.

Around 2:45 A.M., the *Carpathia* was approaching the ice field, and Captain Rostron began to really focus on the waters his own ship was about to enter. For the next half an hour or more, *Carpathia* weaved through a field of ice like a slalom skier—and all in an attempt to save strangers, people no one aboard had ever met.

Think about it, men; he put his own vessel in danger as he reached out to those who were in desperate need.

They arrived at the spot where *Titanic* had been around 4:00 A.M., but now there was no sight of her—other than some items from her that could float. It was too late. A short time later, a flare shot up and the *Carpathia's* crew spotted their first lifeboat, this one containing approximately twenty-five freezing and scared passengers. For the next several hours, she took on over seven hundred passengers from *Titanic's* lifeboats. As daylight arose, it became apparent how dangerous the ice field that *Carpathia* had managed to navigate and that *Titanic* had not, really was. Before he set sail back for New York, Captain Rostron held a short service led by a clergyman to give thanks for the rescued and to remember those who were lost.

There are many lessons we can learn from Captain Rostron's bravery, so let's look at a few. When he first received word of the wreck, he rapidly began to plan, chart, and delegate instructions—while he was dressing.

Dads, here's the question: are we able to do more than one thing at a time with our lives? I know that kind of sounds a bit trite, but the ability to work, build a marriage, raise a successful family, and still have some down time for yourself is a very difficult thing to do. My wife calls it "multi-tasking," something that women sometimes have an easier time doing.

We can't be too surprised that we're cultivating weeds of neglect when we're too focused on our own interests.

The lesson for all of us is that we need to lift our heads out of whatever we are buried in—such as the job, the TV, or whatever else—and pay careful attention to the important areas of our lives. Again, this introspection should lead to making the necessary changes.

The next lesson we can take from Captain Rostron is that he saw the mission that was before them, and he got his crew members focused on the task at hand. He knew not only were they now on a rescue mission, but they were also going to have to pass through some of the same ice fields that had already sunk one ship.

Dads, are you aware yet that there really is a battle for your home? The opposing forces are determined to cause enough damage and destruction to tear it apart. How often do you just sit down with your family and discuss the importance of spending time together? Are we so caught up in all the trappings of this world's system that we fail to communicate with all the members of our families?

> **There really is a battle for your home.**

I recommend some sort of meeting that you lead to lay out the vision, direction, and task at hand for your home. By the way, this might seem incredibly awkward at first, and you might not get the perfect responses you hoped for the first time, but I believe that if you are genuinely honest and consistent with your mission, the chances of your success will increase over time.

Next, Captain Rostron poured all the energy the ship could muster into getting the job done as quickly as possible, and here's the picture: we need to prioritize. There are things in our lives that will slow down our rescue mission. In the case of the *Carpathia*, this meant items as basic as hot water and heat. These are pretty basic necessities, but when you're talking about trying to save lives, even seemingly important things can be cut off for a while in order to accomplish the task.

One of the first things that comes to mind is recreation. Right about now, some of you guys are about to close the book because of this blasphemy, but it's true. Some dads seem to live on the golf course or at the ballpark while mom and the kids wait for you to get done entertaining yourself. And what about the old TV? Many a family has waited in line for some time with dad until a sports event, his favorite show, or the news was over.

What is it, dad, that ensnares your attention so much that it slows down your effort to make a positive mark on your home? We need to have the discipline to throw off the things that slow us down—even when they seem like necessities—in order to come to the rescue of our families.

I'm not against golf and I'm not against television. I really like to play it, and I really like to watch it. I'm simply saying there comes a point in every family where dads need to take the lead role in shutting out and shutting off every influence that isn't a priority and that is trying to drive a wedge into our families.

Don't worry too much; *Carpathia* didn't shut off the heat and hot water permanently; they were turned off only for a short time. You have to urge every ounce of speed in your rescue attempt long enough to rescue those in need. There comes a point where short-term sacrifices have got to be made in order for the long-term health of the home to succeed.

We all should know by now what needs to be switched off, but if you're not sure what they are, go ask your wife and your kids. I promise you *they'll* know.

Once Captain Rostron made his changes and the ship was running with all of its engines at full speed, it caused the decks to throb! Can you picture that? The ship was running so hard, there was a noticeable difference on deck. Now here's the significance: when you really get focused and you make the necessary changes by cutting off some short-term distractions, it will become noticeable to those who know you. They'll sense it, and they'll see it—tangible differences for the good.

It's difficult to hide a positive light in a dark world; people will notice the change in you and in your home. Your golfing buddies will wonder where you are on Saturday mornings and why a family picnic takes precedence over rehashing the same old worn-out high school football stories, and your kids will notice that the TV is turned off and you're now tuned in to their needs. It will make a difference, and while you might lose some time with your buddies or fall behind in your favorite sitcom, your family will notice and can really grow from it.

Another lesson we can all learn from Rostron is that on his way to rescue the passengers, he had to do his best to keep his own ship safe and collision free as he sailed through dangerous waters. He had to keep his own ship protected, and here's the lesson.

We must keep our own hearts in check. I love the book *Wild at Heart* by John Eldredge. It's a challenge for all men to find and guard our own hearts. Eldredge starts out his book on top of a mountain range in search of his heart and does a masterful job throughout the book of challenging men to find and then guard their hearts.

What an incredible challenge! But men, it's got to get done. Probably few of us have conquered this peak, but the prize is worth the fight. It's easy to write about it, but it's another thing to experience it. And one of the ways we'll get there is to make sure our hearts are healthy and sound—not only physically but spiritually and emotionally as well.

The next to the last thing we'll examine is that Captain Rostron finished out what he started to do. What if halfway he just decided that he wasn't going to go any further with the mission? What if he had sailed up to the edge of the ice field, surveyed the situation, and just turned and went in the opposite direction? For all of us the lesson is simple: finish the task. Finish well. Finish what you started.

I have saved the most powerful lesson for the last. When he first was told of the tragedy, some of the first words out of his mouth were, "Tell them we're coming as fast as we can." I've been thinking about who represents the *Titanic* and who represents the *Carpathia*, and I've come to the conclusion that there are several useful analogies here for us to study.

It's obvious that this entire book has been directed at dads and the wake-up call that we need, so the *Carpathia* represents dads coming to the rescue, and the *Titanic* represents families taking on water.

Many fathers are in lifeboats close to the wreck of their families, listening to the cries of their family members as they swim in the icy waters that are swallowing up their dreams. These dads are in need of some serious healing in their own hearts. Some fathers are still aboard their sinking vessels, watching the black waters of the North Atlantic sweep toward them with fatal inevitability. Their vessels are taking on water at such a serious rate that if they don't do something quickly, they're headed to the bottom.

Here is my message to you—those who are in the water or watching it loom close. It's the same message that Captain Rostron transmitted over ninety years ago—*we're coming as quickly as we can to help you.*

I want you to know that if you're seemingly at the end of your rope, hold on because *help is out there.* There are counselors, clergymen, and friends that will help you walk through these difficult days. Your job is to let someone know you're hurting and that you need help—and you need to do it quickly.

And to you men who know of other men who are hurting and are in desperate need for help: your call is to take on the heart of Captain Rostron and reach out to those men before it's too late for them.

I'm writing the last words of this book in the hills of southern Missouri on a family vacation. I've just watched Madison, who is six years old at the writing of this chapter, riding her bike and looking for daddy's approval with her new riding tricks. Her arm has long since healed from the break, yet my heart still carries the scar from my neglect.

Over the two years that I've worked on this project, my own heart has grown stronger with the call to reach out to families—particularly dads—with the message of healing and wholeness because I already possess the former and daily strive to walk in the latter. It can be done in your own heart and hopefully in the hearts of your family—and hopefully you can see your family become whole.

However, you must start somewhere. That day must be today, as you finish this book.

My parting words to those of you who still feel hopeless are these: God can hear your cries for help, and those of us who have heard the call for help are trying to come as fast as we can. Hold on, put into practice the action points you've read in each chapter, and take up the calling by which you've been called—that of being a dad!

FINAL ACTION POINTS

1. Get up before the rest of the family and chart out a course for your home. Make a habit of updating it regularly to stay on the right path!

2. Do you know another father who is in desperate need of help? Try to think of at least one, and make it a point to get active in his life to see him through.

3. Is your wife getting lost in the "busyness" of life and parenthood? If she's been carrying most of the burden, start lifting some of it by offering to take care of some of the family-related issues she's been handling. Also, a weekend or weeklong getaway with just the two of you might sound good to her right about now!

4. Determine to see healing take place in your own heart that came as a result of your own iceberg collision. Set up an appointment and consult someone trustworthy—your pastor, for instance—and talk frankly with him about issues that trouble you regarding being a father. Use him to stay accountable in the future so that you stick with your plan for your healing and that of your family.

AUTHOR CONTACT INFORMATION

Jim Moore

P.O. Box 6310

Springdale, AR 72766

Phone: (479) 751-3535

NOTES

NOTES